The

Home Style Book

The
Home Style Book

Nonie Niesewand

WHITNEY LIBRARY OF DESIGN
an imprint of Watson-Guptill Publications/New York

A QUARTO BOOK

Copyright © 1984 Quarto Publishing Limited
First Published 1984 in the United States by
the Whitney Library of Design,
an imprint of Watson-Guptill Publications, a division of Billboard
Publications, Inc, 1515 Broadway, New York, N.Y. 10036

Library of Congress Catalog number 84-40394

ISBN 0-8230-7272-X

First Printing, 1984

This book was designed and produced by
Quarto Publishing Limited
32 Kingly Court
London W1

Art Editor: Nick Clark
Editor: Emma Johnson-Gilbert
Art Director: Alastair Campbell
Editorial Director: Christopher Fagg
Illustrators: Sotos Achilleous, Stephen Gardiner,
Simon Roulstone, Dave Weeks
Special thanks to: Judy Crammond, Anne Holker,
Lucinda Montefiore, Judy Martin, Deirdre McGarry

Typeset by Leaper & Gard, Bristol
Color origination by Hong Kong Graphic Arts
Service Centre, Hong Kong
Printed and Bound by Poligrafici Calderara SPA,
Bologna, Italy

CONTENTS

SECTION ONE

SECTION TWO

SECTION ONE

ARCHITECTURE AND STRUCTURE
STYLE
COLOR

ARCHITECTURE AND STRUCTURE

In many ways a room that has no architectural features is easier to inject with an individual style than a period piece with niches, cornices and elaborate plaster-work. If you are starting from scratch with a basic box, you can decorate it to your own taste — whether this is minimalist, high-tech or country style. You can even build your own reproduction cornices, fireplaces and mouldings.

In addition to structural details, you should consider what space you will need for furniture and equipment and then plan the layout of the room around this. You will also want to be warm at a price which is not exorbitant and, during a sweltering hot summer, you may want air conditioning.

Even a small house can have a surprising amount of space, but if the rooms seem small, you can perhaps gain height by removing a ceiling and adding beams, or knocking a wall through to make a dining area. Extra windows, new units or a working wall of shelving all make a house appear larger than it actually is.

Begin by working out the function of the room you are going to decorate. Will you eat or entertain in the kitchen? Do you need working space at home? Will the living area also be the sleeping area? The formal living room, the large dining room and the kitchen that is exclusively the cook's domain, are no longer so practical. The open-plan 'design for living' makes better use of smaller space, and impromptu rooms can still be created with the use of movable screens or roller blinds. To function effi-ciently, without stress, it is important to house everything neatly and still have room to walk about — what decorators call 'corridor space'.

It will help you to decide how best to use the space if you draw up a list of the rooms and the furnishings you are housing. Remember that the position of the windows will affect the layout and design of the room. To get away from a formal arrangement of furniture try putting it at right angles. Construct a peninsula with a sideboard, desk or table or use island storage units for TV and hi-fi, to create a room within a room. Sometimes two small sofas can look better than four chairs and an unusual object, such as a large chest, offers storage space, doubling up as an occasional table.

A common problem in modern, custom-built houses is that kitchen units and bathroom fittings have been installed in shapes and colors you would not choose. It is also difficult to make plywood walls, rows of bedroom cupboards, cheap kitchen units, and a 'Pampas' bathroom suite look very stylish. When presented with such an uninspired decor add instant

It took courage as well as style to remodel the interior of a nineteenth-century canal-side house in Herengracht, Holland (**right**). With the period detailing removed, the long narrow room was opened up for contemporary living. Space and light were two immediate gains. An appreciation of the fine construction of the house shows in the sympathetic wall finishes. Original solid load-bearing brick walls (not the cavity walls and expansion joints of modern buildings) were painted white but otherwise left unadorned. In the monochrome room, with its angular modern furniture, textures are important — leather, glass, upholstery and natural wool rugs show to advantage against pale maple floorboards. Open-tread stairs save space and are balanced with bookshelves opposite in the same vertical lines, an exercise in symmetry that adds to the gracious proportions of this interior. Original details and fittings have been lovingly restored in another nineteenth-century house (**left**), first home of David and Sue Leigh in north London. Far from removing original architectural details, they visited demolition sites to find suitable pieces for the renovation of the house. The cast-iron range has a collage of original Victorian tiles on the splashback and hearth. Lacy fans, shells and porcelain displayed on the mantelpiece are in keeping with the old marbled surround. To find out how to marble your own fireplace surround, see page 23.

Starting from scratch
Designers will ask their clients how they intend to use their space. Their answers determine how best to arrange seating, working surface and storage systems. Give yourself some homework before you begin the decoration of a room.

Is there a need to change the wiring or fit dimmer switches?
What heating exists?
Check the water system and the plumbing.
Can the insulation be improved?
What needs restoring or replacing?

These are the structural changes which need careful consideration. Then you can work out how to use your space.

Can the number of rooms needed be provided for with the existing space?

Can you find extra space with loft or basement conversion?

Checklist for action Heating and lighting systems need to be determined first as alteration will hold up decorating. Make sure the room is light and warm. Check architectural details and restore them or add them. Next, prepare the large surface areas like walls, ceilings and floors for decoration. Then consider window treatments, storage systems and furniture.

texture and sound-proofing by putting fabric on the walls. Line them with fabric in a restrained vertical stripe; this makes a good background and gives an optical illusion of height.

Cover the walls first with polyester wadding, stapled directly onto the plywood baseboard and cornice, and then staple over the fabric. For a grander style, you can create a tent effect by taking the fabric up over the ceiling and catching it in the center. A bold treatment involves covering the walls with photographers' silvery reflective cloth, sold by the yard, or glossy PVC, edged with shiny battens along the top and bottom.

If your room is small, do not assume it must be painted white. In an east-facing room, white walls can look grayish and gloomy, unless you add bright, warm colors, such as pinks and apricots, yellows and reds. If you work away from home you will see the liv-

ing room by night most of the time, so you could use dark backgrounds and intense colors with dramatic lighting. Chrome and lacquer fittings, and high-gloss painted ceilings that reflect light will give depth to flimsy walls, as will mirrors and glass shelving.

There are various ways in which you can break up the laminated look in the kitchen. Make an open display unit for cooking utensils and storage jars by removing a couple of cupboard fronts from the wall-mounted units. Put a bold background color behind the shelves, frame the box with picture moldings, and edge the shelves with paper cut-outs. Add a pine dresser or corner cupboard and house your china in it. Hang café curtains from a brass rod, set halfway across the window, and grow some herbs in terracotta pots near the sink. For the kitchen floor, use vinyl tiles (or ceramic tiles if your budget permits) to provide some pattern in the room.

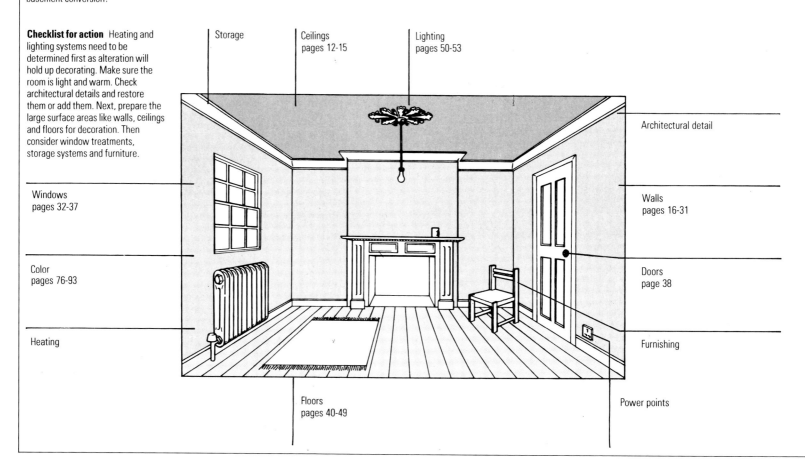

Storage

Ceilings
pages 12-15

Lighting
pages 50-53

Architectural detail

Windows
pages 32-37

Walls
pages 16-31

Color
pages 76-93

Doors
page 38

Heating

Furnishing

Floors
pages 40-49

Power points

Two interiors in modern houses illustrate the proportion and scale in rooms that have no architectural details such as cornices, dados, or fireplaces.

Floor level seating permits a bold ceiling treatment (**above left**). Architect and industrial designer Alan Tye, in his house in Hertfordshire, England, uses dark wood tongue-and-groove boarding with beams across the ceiling, a dramatic contrast to the pale ceramic tiling on the floor. The wooden rail which extends across the window area is emphasized by a woven fabric draped casually over it, drawing the eye level towards the floor cushions and the delicate dried grasses arranged by Swedish-born Mrs Tye.

In this living room (**below left**) a ladder and a cluster of plants are the original accessories that take interest upward from the firm anchorage of bold Art Deco-inspired upholstery covering the three-piece suite. In this harbourview condominium in Greenwich, Connecticut, not only the background is all-white, but also walls and windows, floor and high-gloss ceilings, to reflect the light and create the illusion of space.

CEILINGS

Ceilings can be described as the forgotten feature in most homes, but clever ceiling treatments make all the difference to light and space.

American architect Eric Epstein built in special fittings to this basic bedroom (**right**), papering walls with cream on ivory vine pattern, and leaving floors and ceilings in slatted wood. Downlights set in the ceiling bathe the walls in soft light. The black fireplace, the focus of the room, is emphasized with wooden surrounds.
This fashionably informal kitchen (**far right**) with its open shelves and island unit hung about with cooking utensils, has a fitted ceiling with pine rafters accentuating the height. Even in a small kitchen you can add pine joists supported by wall brackets and upright posts to create a simple pergola for the dining area, or just put in one beam from which to hang your own selection of pots, pans and herbs.

Each decade since World War II has trimmed inches off the standard wall height and today you seldom find high ceilings in modern houses. However, you can make ceilings appear higher by painting them a glossy white and the floor a pale color so that the walls are contained within areas of light. American designer, Noel Jeffrey, has given his living room a golden glow by up-lighting a ceiling covered in 12in (30.4cm) squares of matt-finish gilt tea-paper. You can also lower ceilings dramatically by putting a tongue-and-groove wooden section over the dining area in the kitchen, for example. If you feel that pine is overdone, paint the boards white, or stain them.

An unattractive ceiling can be disguised with miniature beams. Mount polyurethane beams, and bracket them to a strip fastened 4in (10cm) below the ceiling around the perimeter. If you use this structure in the kitchen, you can hang baskets for vegetables and utensils from the beams. Use ceiling track lighting to define areas of interest (see lighting, page 50).

How to paint ceilings
Before you start, rub a small area of the ceiling with a damp cloth. If the powdery surface rubs off easily then the ceiling paper has been painted with distemper. Older ceilings were often painted in this way, but distemper eats through paint rapidly, leaving a welter of blisters. Prepare the surface by soaking it with water, then strip off the paper. When it is dry, fill any cracks and allow it to dry before rubbing it down.

A tented ceiling as formally shaped as this (**top right**) must be cut from a pattern, pinned and seamed before it is stapled to the walls, beginning from the center where light disguises the staples. But covering a ceiling, especially a low one, can be easy if you seam together lengths of fabric — striped sheeting is cheerful and economical — and staple it on without padding underneath.

Create the grand style with a ceiling painting worthy of the Italian Renaissance (**bottom right**). For those wary of tackling such an exacting task, there are wallpapers that will give painterly details to your ceilings.

Finally, give it a coat of emulsion; the first coat should be thinned with water.

Cornices

Polystyrene molding, which has a genuine plaster look when painted, can be sanded to give a smooth finish for painting. The moldings look lightweight, but do not be put off by this; when they are painted they look very effective. They come in lengths of 2.1yds (2m), and you can make up your own cornice design, using the pre-cut mitred corners, zig-zag pieces and curved moldings to frame the ceiling. Filler glue, recommended by the manufacturer should be used to set the cornice strips easily in place. Press it on with your hands and wipe away any excess glue with a damp sponge.

Ceiling centers, also molded with polystyrene come in three shapes — oval, round, or diamond — and measure from about 2in to 2ft (6cm to 60cm) in diameter. A good anchor for an overhead light in a more traditional room, these can be fitted easily over the centerpiece light by removing the bulb and sliding the wire through the central hole.

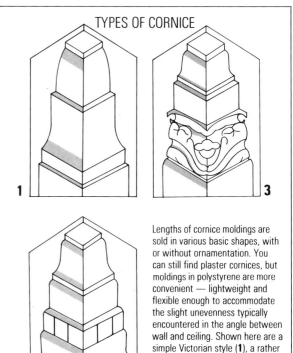

TYPES OF CORNICE

1

3

2

Lengths of cornice moldings are sold in various basic shapes, with or without ornamentation. You can still find plaster cornices, but moldings in polystyrene are more convenient — lightweight and flexible enough to accommodate the slight unevenness typically encountered in the angle between wall and ceiling. Shown here are a simple Victorian style (**1**), a rather more sculptured Edwardian type (**2**) and one elaborated with classical acanthus leaf patterning (**3**).

Bamboo poles (**left**) are light and effective as a ceiling covering, though not as easy to apply as their lightness suggests. To fix long bamboo poles horizontally, you will have to drill screw holes through the already split bamboo halves with an electric drill. Putting nails into the poles will only split them further. In this room white walls and a turquoise carpet give an Indonesian feeling to the room, emphasized by the peacock chair, bowls of feathers and the ivory screen set in the wall. To give the illusion of further bamboo accessories you can paint on a bamboo-like finish. Decorator Diana Phipps painted aluminum rods to resemble bamboo, to replace missing stair rods, with a color she terms 'a cross between parchment and lightwood'. Yellow ocher mixed with a dab of Vandyke brown, diluted with plenty of turpentine, is washed on rather than stippled. Raw umber simulating knuckles, or an occasional smudged line of raw umber helps the illusion. When dry, the paint finish is sealed with semi-matt polyurethane. Decorator Elizabeth Eaton uses split bamboo rods to make dado rails in her London shop, anchoring the base with a strong colour and using a patterned paper above.

WALLS

Walls, by their sheer expanse, offer the most exciting design possibilities in every room, in their own right and in a supporting role.

If you are using white paint for walls with an uneven surface, consider giving them texture by first putting up yachting canvas as a background for paint. Alternatively, use clear primary colors for upholstery, furnishing, and accessories to pull the eye away from blank walls. On white walls with an even surface you could delineate the whiteness with bands of color along the baseboards and around door frames. Use a wallpaper border around the edge that joins the wall and the ceiling. A dado rail, running around the room at windowsill height and marked with a border paper or your own stencil, will lower the ceiling visually and pull the room together. Areas of the wall above these horizontal demarcation lines could be treated in a different way, with a change of color or pattern — a scheme that will balance the room and break up the vertical lines. In a room with good proportions, you could paint paneling below the dado rail in shades darker than the wall color (just stir raw umber into an oil-based paint to darken it). Classicists will marble the panels, country house enthusiasts will stencil them.

Mirrors

A certain luminosity can be created in all-white rooms by using mirrors to good effect. This can be an expensive way of gaining light and the illusion of space, but cheap alternatives do exist in the form of glass mosaic, shiny paint, lacquer, foil or mirrorlite (plastic sheeting substitute), all of which give a similar effect. By cover-

Different wall treatments can draw attention to interesting features, or disguise the true dimensions of a room. Strong color will advance walls, pale tints seem to push them back.
Alcoves set at different heights (**left**) follow the diagonal height of the stairs. Both features lead naturally from one level to the next. Patterns of light and shade from aluminum slatted blinds reflect on steely prefabricated walls (**above**). Architects Patty and Michael Hopkins' modular frame metal and glass house in London uses blinds inside to create opaque 'walls' and to screen glass elevations to the garden.
Black Venetian blinds (**right**) create bold horizontal lines, the pastel yellow struts giving vertical interest that visually heightens the distance from floor to ceiling. In this exercise in geometry, the rounded edges of the plexiglass table, the curving outline of the cast-iron staircase painted white and the egg all help to break the line.

ing an entire wall with mirrors, you can visually double the space in the room, but remember that not all buildings have walls strong enough to hold heavy mirrors. The Art Deco enthusiast will cover doors with mirrors, put mirror tiles on tabletops and use thin strips of mirror to edge the tops of walls below the ceiling. Small mirror tiles are also effective around a fireplace, where they will catch the light from flickering flames. A novel way to give a small room perspective is to replace the glass in a window with no view with a mirror panel, or put mirrors on the wall opposite a scenic window to bring the view into the room.

Pictures

If you possess an undistinguished collection of framed graphics, hang them in groups to detract attention from any one piece; consider putting them on to colored mounts that will pick up the colors of scatter cushions and fabrics. Try out groupings of pictures by sticking double-sided tape on the backs of old cards and moving a selection of images around until you obtain the desired effect. If you favor a streamlined, minimalist interior, you will probably prop your pictures against the wall so that they are at the right level for the cushion seating and bedding rolls.

How to paint walls

Any structural changes that have to be made, such as rewiring for dimmer switches, mean that plasterwork

Three very diffent wall surfaces are used to create interest in these rooms — plates, mirrors and wooden squares.

A wall of plates (**far left**) bought in junk shops makes a natural progression to the dresser, painted in high gloss blue and varnished, that serves as a bold frame for a mainly blue and white collection of china.

Mirrored walls (**center**) stretches space without interruption, making this small study space seem larger and doubling the image of the Oriental rug, the one splash of color in the design. The persoectives are sharpened by the two arches that link this study to the adjoining room. To keep the illusion of space, the background is a restrained mixture of white and natural woods, with a dash of red in the lampshade and rug, and the fresh contrast of green plants.

Bold red underfoot and overhead in this spacious bedroom (**left**) works as a decorative scheme largely because of the link formed by wooden panels on the walls, giving a honeyed glow that suggests opulence and the patina of age. Chipboard panels bought at a materials supply house can be rubbed over with a commercial woodstain applied in soft swirls, then sealed with a matt varnish, before being battened to the wall. Against this dramatic background, the windows are less conspicuous, toned down with pinoleum blinds and white curtains that are echoed in the cool simplicity of the white bed linen.

Wall and ceiling surfaces show all the weathering that a house withstands. Today these watermarks are becoming a status symbol, an intrinsic sign to the cognoscenti that no building inspector's approval was needed to either condone, or condemn, the house. Architect Piers Gough, for example, has some vintage watermarks and damp stains as part of the decorative scheme in his waterhouse London home.

This bedroom (**right**), designed by Martex in the United States of America, has a similar stylish ceiling with great brushstrokes of distemper giving texture to the ceiling. Ceilings that are distempered need to have the distemper rubbed off with a wet rag until no trace remains, otherwise the lime in the distemper will eat up any paint applied over it.

remains damp and painting has to be postponed. For a high-gloss finish, which means applying an oil-based paint, you will have to wait a year. Happily, emulsions which are water-based, and allow plaster to breathe can be applied the week after. A mix of filler should be applied to any cracks, and allowed to dry, then sanded down and dusted down vigorously before painting. The first coat of emulsion should be thinned with water to aid penetration. Never paint over flaking or chipped areas of plaster, but sand them down after scraping. A medium-grade sandpaper will give the new paint a textured base. In kitchens and bathrooms, the tougher silk paints need to go over really dry plaster so it is probably worth waiting, rather than applying a water-based emulsion.

If you are using lining paper, it is easier to paint over old wallpaper rather than tackle the messy job of stripping it off. If the paper is patterned test a little of the color to make sure that the background paper does not stain through wet paint. On poor quality wall surfaces, you will have to apply lining paper or you might consider a textured paint which will camouflage them. Apply the paper with a roller that has a trellis pattern embossed on it or with a spatula and sponge. Experiment first on spare hardboard sheets.

Plaster surfaces are generally of a very low standard these days, and it helps to disguise this with a rougher paint finish. Dabbing the paint on with a soft sponge will give an agreeable dappled finish. Use a slightly deeper shade for the second coat and it will come up like parchment paper.

Sound paintwork that is to be painted a different color merely needs washing down with a decorator's detergent, then rinsing with clear water. When this has dried, rub down with medium-grade sandpaper.

6. Use a roller along the seams to make sure that they cling to the wall.

7. Never try to wrap paper round the corners; cut it off at the corner and match up the next length.

8. Unscrew fittings for plug sockets and light switches, having switched off the mains supply first. Now is the time to consider replacing them with new finishes in bold primary colors or brass fittings.

9. Cut the paper round the indentation and screw back the fittings over the edges.

Papering a ceiling

Fitting ceiling paper is more difficult than hanging wallpaper, so it is a good idea to enlist some help for this task. You should always start papering from the main window, moving in towards the center of the ceiling.

1. Chalk a piece of string and use it to mark a guideline for the first length of paper.

2. Measure the paper, allowing for a small overlap at each end, as with wallpaper.

3. Paste and fold the paper, concertina-style (see instructions below).

4. For hanging the paper, face the wall and peel back each fold in turn, pressing it to the ceiling.

5. At a ceiling light fitting cut a cross in the paper with a pair of scissors and peel the corners back. Go back and trim the paper around the light when you have fitted the rest of the strip.

Folding the paper (left)

Place the paper, paste-side up, on the table. Fold one end over about 12in (30cm). Lift this piece clear and fold another section 24in (68cm). Turn the first piece back onto the second so that you are folding in a zigzag fashion. Continue in this way (the last piece should be folded 12in/30cm). For ease of handling, lay the paper over a wooden roller or wallpaper roll (**above**) and hold the folds in your hand.

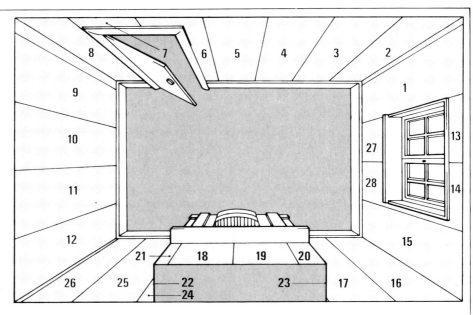

The surfaces can be leveled with a little primer and some filler. At baseboard level, use masking tape along the edges or a decorator's rule to prevent wobbly edges. An obvious point, often overlooked when painting walls, is that you should paint the trims before you paint the outer walls.

When painting paneled doors, start with the inside panels, do cross bars in the center next, and finally the outer edges. Ideally, interior woodwork should be covered with an undercoat, followed by one or two coats of gloss finish, but you can just use two coats of a gloss or oil-based silk. Allow two days for it to dry.

Wallpapers

The latest range of wallpaper has moved away from the coordinated kits that match the wallpaper with the fabric and paint color. This trend has been superseded by wallpapers that exactly duplicate the paint finishes of dragging, scumbling, stippling and marbling, but with more finesse. You can even add stenciled borders that have the same background finishes as the main paper, an easy alternative for those who do not have the courage, or the time, to apply complicated techniques to painted walls. These are not cheap but they are more durable than the cheaper papers that tear easily when hung.

Buying papers by the roll

Standard wallpapers come in rolls approximately 11yds (10m) long x 21in (53cm) wide. To calculate the

Order of papering

Begin at one side of the window and work out in an anti-clockwise direction (**1-12**). Measure and cut the small sections for above the window (**13, 14**) and when these have been put up, work away from the window on the other side (**15-17**). At a fireplace, stick the center panels first (**18, 19**) and the others on either side (**20, 21**), fitting them carefully into the corners (**22, 23**). Finally, fit the two panels beneath the window frame (**27, 28**). Always try to avoid overlapping lengths of paper; when you do have to (at corners, for example) overlap towards the light so that the join of the paper does not cast a shadow.

number of rolls required for ceilings and walls, please refer to the charts on pages 212 and 213. The larger patterns need more paper to allow for matching. Always start with the pattern at the top, at cornice height, and cut it at the base. With some of the plainer papers, especially hand-finished ones like those from Coles and Sandersons, make sure that you have the same batch number as colors vary and a bad match will show when it is pasted to the walls. Textured papers like burlap and bark often come in different widths so you will have to give the room measurements to the shop when ordering.

Heavy duty vinyls that can be scrubbed and sponged do not work very well in living areas, unless you have a high-tech decor with bold colors and plenty of plexiglass and plastic. If you choose a paper that is not classified as heavy duty for washing down, brush on a protective coat of matt finish afterwards.

Borders

Imaginative borders can make an ordinary room look stylish. Buy them to complement the wallpaper, or use them with plain painted surfaces to outline cornices, doors, baseboards or create separate areas for dado rails or picture rails. If you are not matching a border to a wallpaper but intend using it to make an undistinguished room more interesting, then buy the border first and match the paint color to it. Grecian key designs will give a certain formality, or the cottagy stencils of fruit and flowers in baskets, of which there are many examples, duplicate hand painting but with less effort.

The better quality papers require two pastings with size, but leave them for five minutes between coats so that a tacky base forms before pasting up. Elizabeth Eaton, interior decorators, have an imposing harlequin diamond pattern paper in the entrance to their London shop. It is broken at dado height and at cornice level with bamboo strips, split in half and nailed to the wall — an effective way of creating a border on a wallpaper base.

Wallpapers that emulate decorative paint finishes:
Osborne and Little (**1-5**)
Laura Ashley (**6**)
John Oliver (**7**)
Margo International (**8**)
Tissunique (**9**)
Designer's Guild (**10**)
Arthur Sanderson & Sons Ltd (**11, 12**)

Wallpaper manufacturers have recognized the commercial potential of papers that copy the fashionable appeal of expensive and elaborate paint finishes. Dragged, scumbled, rag-rubbed, stenciled, marbled and stippled wall finishes are reproduced in a range of papers. So if your amateur effort at daubing on paint fails to capture the professional finish of the original model, look to these new wallpapers for a quick cover-up.

Trompe l'oeil, the art of deception with 3-D painting on the walls, is beyond the skills of most home decorators. Yet this neo-Palladian entrance (**above**) was entirely created by Osborne and Little using only their wallpapers cut into different shapes to suggest stairs and grand details. Even the view is fake. Balustrades painted directly onto the wallpaper and curtain drapes complete the stage set. Anyone with scissors and a paste table could follow this scheme to recreate a grand classical entrance against dull, flat wall.

WINDOWS AND DOORS

A focus of attention inside and out, windows and doors deserve to be given original treatment.

Now that the walls and ceiling of your room have been decorated to your taste, take time to look out of the windows. If privacy — or the view — is a problem, you will have to devise a scheme which conceals or minimizes it without blocking the light. Color is dependent on light and the light will be different in each room, according to the number and size of the windows, the aspect of the room and any obstruction to the light. Just as each piece of furniture needs to be pushed about in the room before the correct place is found for it, so a piece of material can be very helpful when you are trying out window-dressing. Resist shrouding the windows in sheers of fabric, unless you can achieve a sort of careless neo-Palladian grace by scarving rods and valances with billowing lengths of material, knotted at the ends and looped into swags. Dutch interior designer, Lidewij Edelkoort, used linen drapes to conceal a bathroom boiler in a Paris apartment, and a Bedouin tent lining to creat a seat in her study.

To use fabrics to best effect at the window, you need to understand the scale and proportion of your rooms. The current enthusiasm for grand fabric drapes at perfectly ordinary windows has obscured the point that windows are for letting in light, and for giving height to the room. Festoons can look marvelous, either teamed in a light-hearted way with conventional gathered curtains, as Caroline Arbor the photographer has done in her country cottage (see page 65), or used to screen a view of terraced houses as David Mlinaric has done in his kitchen (page 174). If you have a splendid view, you can draw attention to it by putting ceramic tiles around the window frame and stapling fabric into the surrounds. A cheerless room without a view could be enlivened by using mirrors to reflect the opposite wall. To provide privacy, without blocking out the light, improvise with a grille across the window. Perforated hardboard in latticework is a lightweight imitation of the fifties' fashion for grilles cast in concrete, popularized by American architect, Edward Durrell Stone.

You can gather information and ideas on more traditional methods of window-dressing from old books, such as *The Victorian Upholsterers' Pattern Book* at the Victoria and Albert Museum in London. If pins, tucks and pleats seem too much like hard work, try doing it the way real window dressers do, with a staple gun, ribbons and real silk. Curtains like those seen in pictures of nineteenth-century ceremonial apartments can be re-created using inexpensive dress fabrics, such as denim, with a quilted lining and ribbed

Two grand window treatments, both suggested by the shape of the windows:

The curved lines of the original window frame in a London house (**far left**) inspired the cascade that masks the valance. A muslin template was hung from the track to achieve the exact shape. Chintz striped in maize, white, pink and turquoise is lined and interlined for the formal drapes. Original shutters were first painted with a cream eggshell base, then dragged with a blue scumble glaze.

A glassed-in and roofed extension to a formal eighteenth-century house (**left**) suggested an extra dining alcove to decorator Diana Phipps. She copied the window shape from an old mirror. As the alcove has a lower ceiling and is not as wide as the room, it was covered in a different material to stress its separateness. Around the windows and the ceiling she stapled Indian crewelwork bedspreads to suggest a pavilion and screened the glass panes with Holland blinds that pull up from the base instead of down from the arch and are hidden when not in use by the cushions on the denim-covered sofa.

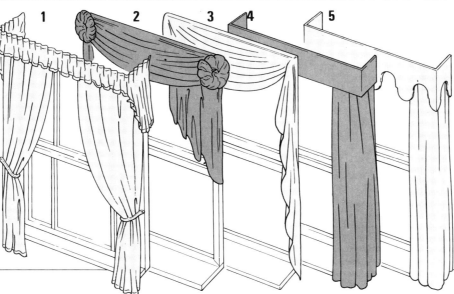

A valance is a neat complement to the soft framing of a window that the curtains provide (**left**). You can choose a gently pleated or draped fabric valance, or a stiff construction of wood or buckram. Evenly gathered fabric looks well with tie-back curtains (**1**). A swag, trailing at the sides, can be finished with fabric rosettes (**2**). Simple draping of a fine, flowing fabric produces an elegant effect (**3**). A hard valance can be a plain, straight box shape (**4**) or cut with scallops or crenelations on the lower edge (**5**). to emphasize the vertical drop.

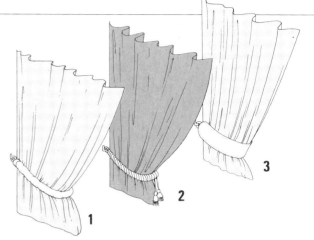

Daphne and Joss Graham, who travel in Turkey and India buying textiles, flat weaves and rugs for their London shops, hung camel reins around their kitchen window (**above**) to frame a Habitat pinoleum blind stained blue. An Afghan tent band is pinned up to form the cornice — 'Use braids or borders to suggest cornices rather than let walls just stop abruptly' advises Daphne Graham who, as assistant to a director of Colefax and Fowler, was responsible for coordinating the schemes for some of Britain's grandest houses. She uses old textiles decoratively and to suggest architectural details. She believes

stripped wood can look pretentious and gloomy, so doors. architraves, baseboards, shutters and all woodwork in the three-bedroomed London house are painted white, as white reflects the light.

Tiebacks (above right) are used to let the maximum amount of daylight into the room, as well as to frame the window. You can use cords (**1** and **2**), hat ribbon, silk ribbons, webbing, or leather thongs to tie curtains back. More formal fabric tie-backs (**3**) are less flexible, but more suitable for heavy drapes that need firm anchorage.

binding looped and twirled along the edges to make it more luxurious. Full-length curtain drapes do not have to be too formal as long as the effect is sumptuous. For the fresh, country-cottage look you can frill the edges of pieces of gingham, or draw a café curtain across the windows. Curtains that reach only as far as the sill are not very attractive, but you could emphasize the window with a window seat below, and cover the window sill with a quilted cushion top.

Daphne Graham, decorator and owner of a rug shop, uses a mixture of Colefax and Fowler formal chintzes with Afghan rugs, Turkish pantaloons and Indian embroideries at the window of her Victorian house in London. In place of valances she uses upholsterers' rope, or Rajasthani camel drivers' reins in brilliantly colored silk and wool, and loops and twirls it into shapes above the curtains or shutters.

Nothing looks more uninspired than a wall-to-wall line-up of curtains that are made to measure. If you inherit acres of them, try jazzing them up with real silk ribbon, tied at intervals along the line-up. You can advance this theme with red ribbon parcel tags, peeled off and stuck above pictures hung on the walls. From scraps of old chintzes and glazed cottons, cut out the flowers, fruit baskets or garlands and sew or glue them on to a plain background material in the same color as the chintz, or stick a wallpaper border or stencil cuts around the window.

Valances

If the top of the curtain is hidden by a valance you can always improvise a grand drape; padding a valance improves the look of it immediately. Cut the padding to size, then cut the fabric cover larger than the valance shape, with notches at strategic points, and

glue it to the back of the valance.

Any three-sided frame, set well away from the curtain rod or track and attached to a batten, can hold drapes in cascades, festoons, swags or swoops, but these treatments really only suit grand windows. Swags are the simplest to make — they consist of a straight piece of material with a curved base and sides cut slightly on the bias. Hem the curved part, gather or pleat the sides and staple them into place. You can attach two swags to the center of a valance, hiding the join with a straight strip of material.

You can always replace a valance with an unusual curtain heading. For example, set a line of ruffles above the curtains in a country cottage, or cover the curtain track with a ruffle, stiffened with interlining, so that it sticks up above the track, against the wall. This idea was used by Pat Drummond of Rumson in New Jersey to surround the coral drapes that frame her window seat. She used a Provencal blue sprigged fabric for the seat and bits and pieces of old American quilts for scatter cushions.

Tracks and rods

The simplest curtains of all are lengths of fabric attached to wooden rings and strung on a rod. For the latest in curtain rods, use some 1½in (3.3cm) plastic PVC plumbing pipe. This is wider than normal rods and much cheaper. Sand the lengths of pipe and spray paint them, or make a tube at the end of your fabric and slip the rod into it. Use PVC plumbing elbows to support the rod.

Brass rods with finials and brass rings, and wooden rods and rings come in varying widths. Remember, the thicker the rings, the less far back the curtains will draw so buy longer rods if you need all the light you

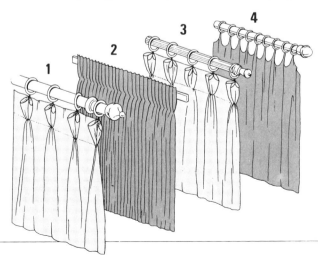

Headings for curtains (left) come in several different styles and you can choose the one to suit your taste or the weight of the fabric. Double pinch pleats (**1**) gather the fabric into neat folds. Pencil pleats (**2**) are much tighter and require more fabric — three times the length of the curtain track. You can create more luxurious folds with triple pinch pleats (**3**) which can be pulled across with a drawcord, woven into the tape. For a much lighter look, use sheers (**4**), such as muslin, net or lace, clipped into rings on a rod. These can just hang, or the material can be caught up in a swag.

Conventional triple pinch-pleat curtain headings (**above**) separate the dining alcove from the living area in this English country house. A white curtain rod emphasizes the alcove area, used not only to support the curtains, in all the colors of 'High Summer' from Sanderson fabrics, but also to suspend over the table its unusual centerpiece, the varnished paper umbrella that unfurls above the giant peonies in a vase. A light bulb could be hung in the umbrella for central light with unique style. A low coffee table is provided by the mahogany chest that doubles up as storage space for a record

collection. Lilian Delavorya's watercolor has all the sunny colors and peachy tones appropriate for this setting.

can get, and draw back the curtains to the walls on either side. Aluminum tracks can be easily bent to turn corners, a great advantage in houses with bays. Use tracks with matt finish in the same colors as the wall finish above the window. Allow 1½ft (46cm) each side when ordering the track. The fuller the curtains, the more you need to extend the track (see page 212 for measurements).

Blinds

Just as interior decorators love the effect of elegant drapes, so designers and architects prefer the simplicity of blinds or screens which allow plenty of light to enter a room. This appreciation of blinds was shown to good effect at the Ideal Home exhibition in London. For the first time a variety of blinds were displayed at every window, instead of curtains. Ordinary roller blinds can be made at home from a kit. Almost any material can be used with the fabric stiffener that accompanies these 'Holland blind' kits. The Roman blind, which looks like an ordinary blind when down but pulls up into a neat series of pleats, is sometimes emphasized with wooden battens tucked into the tubes at the back, like battens in sails. Vertical blinds work on the same principle and have sophisticated mechanisms to ensure easy opening and closing. The festoon blind looks best if only the sides are gathered and it is left half-drawn so that the flounces can be seen properly. Few of these blinds are designed for regular pulling up and down. The most sophisticated type of blind is the Venetian blind, multi-colored, or with a matt finish or mirror surface.

Screens

If you buy a small folding screen, you can stand it beneath the window to hide an ill-placed radiator panel and place it on the window sill at night to provide privacy. Make an improvised dressing room area in a bedroom with a homemade screen. Thread patterned sheets on to elastic at the top and bottom and put them on to a frame. These frames were popular in the nineteenth century and you can pick them up in junk shops. In the living room, paint the frame with three coats of matt black, put high gloss on top then tack in large scale fabrics.

Shutters

Older houses have splendid wooden shutters which should never be removed. Apart from looking good, they are very secure and provide a certain amount of protection against break-ins. For cosmetic reasons

Two rooms employing shock tactics at window level: one window is lavishly festooned in coral, the other makes an exercise in modernist restraint.

Festoon blinds (**above**) look best at a large window with a long drop, rather than a wide swathe. In this idiosyncratic room with its richness of pattern and color, the ornately gilded cornice has been cut away to house a modern track. The lavish blind has a pleated heading and is edged with fringes as wide as the bullion fringes of the button-back sofas.

Cool modernism is applied in this black, white and gray interior of an Amsterdam house (**right**). Black lacquer table, black cord covered chair, white unit to house electronic equipment — even the radiator panel is painted gray. So the sunny yellow blinds at the window not only focus attention on the single source of natural daylight in this industrial scheme but add a genuinely cheerful note to the room.

Top right: (**1**) Festoon or Austrian blind (**2**) Roller blind (**3**) Vertical louver blind (**4**) (Pinoleum blind — bamboo blinds are similar in style (**5**) Roman blind (**6**) Venetian blind

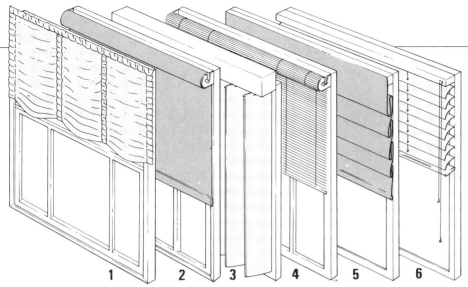

1   2   3   4   5   6

only, you could construct lightweight shutters, made from foam insulation boards. Use picture frame moldings for glue-on panels and hinges. Designer Sybil Levine used these shutters to conceal an entire wall of glass in a Manhattan apartment. As it was rented no structural alterations could be made. The advantage of shutters is that they can be made almost any size to elongate or widen the window area, as long as they do not have to be drawn together. Redolent of the American Deep South are the wooden slatted shutters, called Plantation shutters. These have movable slats which can be set up in tiers on high windows and they can be stained or painted any color to match a scheme.

Doors

Doors are seldom considered in the decorating scheme, yet they take up a considerable amount of space in a room. You will need to leave about 7sq ft (2.1m, squared) clear for opening the door into a room and this space can be critical in a small bedroom, bathroom or kitchen.

Conventional double doors that do not project into a room in the same way that a single door does, can save up to 40 percent floor space. Half-width saloon doors, called bi-folds, can save 6sq ft (1.8m, squared) as they are hinged together for folding away at the sides. Ordinary hinges are adequate for these, although the more expensive models have metal alignment plates to keep the joint flat when the door is closed.

Concertina doors that fold into each other like an accordion come in colored PVC to fit in with the decor of a high-tech bathroom, or in hard or soft wood, obtained from builders' stores. To get the correct sliding mechanism you will need a metal track for the door frame. This can be screwed underneath the top with hooks for wheeled hangers. The concertina door, the multifold door, or the louvered bifolds in wood are the best room dividers as sliding and double doors can be too cumbersome.

The modern unpaneled flat door could probably do with dressing up to disguise the flimsy veneered surface. If it is the front door, you could add a shell fanlight, made from lightweight plaster pieces that can be glued together according to a manufacturer's diagram. Some of these designs were inspired by details from grand architecture, such as the eighteenth-century Royal Pavilion at Brighton with its trellis and shell moldings. When these moldings are painted white and given a final finish they take on an

authentic look. If there is no light in the hall, add panes of glass to fit in with the moldings, or fit a panel of glass above the door.

Letterboxes should be large enough to take heavy-duty envelopes and magazines, but not so large that a burglar can fit an arm inside to open the front door. The recommended height for a letterbox on the front door is 2ft 6in (76.3cm) minimum and 4ft 9in (1.45m) maximum. The new brass letterboxes that screw into the door on a bolt, come in a variety of period styles; old brass or cast-iron letterboxes can be cleaned up in an acid bath. Hardware stores stock selections of door knockers, numbers and enameled plates that will improve the external appearance of your door.

The inside doors of a modern apartment can be improved with a door handle from the Italian plastic range, in simple shades and bold colors, or anodized aluminum handles. If you are a skillful hand at painting

you can add a few amusing touches to a door, such as a hand above the knocker, or a message spelt out in elegant Letraset. The more sophisticated artist can tackle *trompe l'oeil* on completely flat doors that are painted white. Paint in the recessed panels with mid-sheen paint that is tinted a greenish grey with raw umber, add darker lines to two sides to suggest shadows in the panels. Widen the panels on narrow doors to compensate for the lack of breadth and to make the door appear better proportioned. Use masking tape when painting to keep the edges straight. In the space above the door, you can paint a fanlight in grisaille (the same color, made gray with raw umber or lightened with white). Painting the door frames a bold color will merely emphasize the flatness of the doors, so this is only a good idea if you have stylish handles and a good view behind the door to add another dimension to a one-dimensional entrance.

These four doors illustrate the art of making an entrance. Turquoise Art Nouveau glass panels (**far left**), the color of Islamic tiles, add to the unexpected pattern in this room dancing with lights and colors set against a neutral background. Stained glass panels in a well proportioned door (**left**) can visually increase the height or width of the door. Stained glass is having a contemporary revival.
Sometimes the front door is overlooked as a decorative element. The startled cat among the milk bottles (**above**) makes a witty suburban statement, simply executed in black and white gloss paint on red.
Well-painted birds and flamingos, in designs inspired by the old East India chintzes, grace these door panels (**right**), a deliberate contrast in their delicacy and craftsmanship to the original rough floorboards and modern graphics.

FLOORS

Floors are often the victims of a hasty cover-up, but there are many different ways of improving on the bare essentials.

Uniform floors in the cheapest available flooring material are the hallmark of houses built in the past decade. Drab, wall-to-wall carpets, usually of the poorest quality, muffle the concrete floors and floorboards.

The right floor covering can be practical as well as stylish; the wrong one requires careful treatment to prevent it from looking shabby. Often this relates to color choice: how many urban children creep in stockinged feet around the house because their parents invested in that good old stand-by, the cream or maize carpet? Floors should be hardy, as well as good looking. Advice to first-time buyers at the Spring '84 Ideal Home exhibition in London was that they should buy quality carpeting, even if it was more expensive. If you want a cut pile carpet for the living room, pure wool is the most expensive, but wool/synthetic mixes, synthetic cut pile or cord, or bonded carpet — pile fiber bonded to a backing — are cheaper alternatives.

Remember that the floor covering must be appropriate to the function of the room. Wood, brick or tile can be used throughout the house, whereas carpets are limited to living rooms, bedrooms and stairs as they can be a nuisance in bathrooms and kitchens. Consider such factors as wear and tear, traffic, warmth, safety and sound-proofing. The kitchen floor should be easy to clean but not too slippery, halls and stairs need a hard-wearing material and bedrooms should be cosy, although you may prefer to use a more practical floor covering in a child's room which is also a playroom.

Carpets

Most carpets are graded according to their quality. For example grade D is general wear for living rooms and halls; grades E and F are suitable for bedrooms. How carpets stand up to use is determined by the type and the amount of fiber packed into the pile. Tufts should be densely packed with little or no backing visible when you bend back the carpet. A carpet should always be fitted professionally and a good underlay is essential unless you have a carpet with its own foam backing.

If you plan to carpet a small apartment (a good way of sound-proofing), use the same carpet throughout to unify it. In more roomy houses you can vary the carpeting. Remember that carpets with high pile and long tufts are more susceptible to wear and tear in a heavy traffic area, so a carpet with lower pile would be more suitable in a corridor.

When choosing the color of your carpet, you will

Original ideas for different textures to be trampled underfoot: an expensive designer solution to a small space, running a wall-to-wall carpet with diagonal stripes in a bold magenta, and a cheap, casual floor covering anchored artistically to give a spacious, informal room a sense of permanence.

In the decorator's show house (**left**) designed by American Harvey Herman, the fine line of magenta weave in the wall-to-wall carpet alters the perspectives of a small living room. Notice that the quilted webbing stripes on the floor cushions run in the opposite direction.

April Geirman's jokey interpretation of the traditional principle of the front room with everything under wraps (**above**). The underfelt is covered with dust sheets, anchored with drawing pins and stone sculptures shaped like boulders. Canvas and chrome chairs are attended by the ever-present bell boy, a wooden cutout presenting a salver as a tiny occasional table. Overhead is the 'Giraffe' suspension light designed by Shiu Kay Khan. There are no fabrics or shutters to interfere with the natural light streaming in from the well proportioned windows.

This Californian house (**right**), built to maximize small space measures only 20ft (6.1m) by 40ft (12.2m) by 20ft (6.1m), with a window to increase the illusion of space. Upstairs is a guest loft 20ft (6.1m) square. Architect Steven Ehrlich used stucco over a wooden frame to build the house. An intelligent decorating scheme, anchored in the firm use of pastel colors creates a feeling of spaciousness. The only pattern introduced into this small room is the modern graphics of the rug. Simple wicker furniture, with upholstered cushions in white with black piping, has the same sea-green accents that are found in the rug border. While this rug is a special purchase, the enthusiastic decorator with no spare cash can design a geometric floor pattern painted directly onto natural canvas backing with fabric-dye felt pens. American painter and fabric artist Peter Fasano searched for a decorating look that would be quick, inexpensive, and light in feeling — perfect for summer homes and his answer was to paint over classical sisal and maize rugs. Brushes, sponges, or small rollers dipped into acrylic paints will imprint the color upon the rugs. He advises using an oil-based paint if the rugs are going to get heavy wear. If necessary, the designs can be touched up with a brush to cover wear and tear. Use your imagination to create striking patterns as simple as the geometrics shown here.

probably be given little samples, but it is difficult to imagine what these look like over a large area. It is better to buy a few yards which you can spread out near the fabric you like and see how the light in your room affects the tone. Look at the color in daylight before basing your color scheme on it. Rooms which get plenty of sunshine during the day tend to look warmer and can take cooler blues, green, and lilac — colors which give the illusion of space. Bleaker rooms that face north or east need cheering up with warm tans, chocolate or coral.

The inevitable changeability of contemporary living has deterred many homeowners from laying carpets in their houses. Instead there is a much wider use of less permanent, inexpensive floor covering, such as easy-to-place rugs or the new vinyls that so grandly imitate marble finishes.

Rugs

You can always use rugs to give a different emphasis of colour to a room, and the advantage of these for contemporary living is that they can be moved around to fit a change of scheme. They are also easy to place and immensely decorative.

Rugs provide a wealth of design possibilities — they serve to break up an uninterrupted expanse of floor or carpet, to define furniture groupings within a space and they can fit beautifully into the atmosphere of a period room. When putting down rugs avoid placing a series of tiny rugs in a large room, and leave large, densely patterned rugs out of a small one. If you have a generously proportioned room, you could try using pattern upon pattern, a technique perfected by Daphne Graham (pages 108-109) who owns a rug shop in London. In her home she puts together many different rugs — rag rugs from Poland, Afghan eating rugs and Caucasian kelims with tent lining runners overlapping the edges. Pattern enlivens a room, but printed fabrics and highly patterned rugs can be tricky unless you make a selection based on color combinations.

Dhurries

A dhurrie rug is a flat woven carpet that comes from India. Traditionally cotton striped in rather bold colors, now they are available in the newest pastels and patterns. Originally a dhurrie served as the bottom layer for a quilted bedding roll, becoming the daytime sleeping bag cover for the roll, but in palaces it lined the corridors of the *dhurbar* (assembly) hall where petitioners waited patiently to see the ministers. Bed-sized dhurries, in earthy vegetable dyes and

Daphne Graham, owner of the Rug Shop in London, shows off her collection of flat weaves and rugs with the background of a simple terracotta quarry tile, in fact a cushion-backed vinyl, in the kitchen/dining area of her London house (**above**). The dining table is covered with a Turkish Gigim in an unusual check, the wall hanging is an eighteenth-century Thracian kelim now worn threadbare but showing vestiges of its past delicacy and splendor. The rug underfoot is a North Western Persian kelim, dating from the nineteenth century, in sand, coral and turquoise on a white background. A Chinese coolie's hat has been turned into a simple lampshade above the table.

broad stripes, are still made in the villages of northern India, but the enthusiasm of decorators David Hicks and Mary Fox Linton for the carpet designs of Bombay manufacturer, Shyam Ahuja, has led to some innovations in pale pastels. The newest dhurries are woven in wool, in blue and white zig-zag stripes, in stars and diamonds, crosses and chevrons, diagonals and cross-stitch florals, all according to the traditional warp and woof of the village looms. The traditional dhurries do exist, but they are collectors' items as they received so much hard wear in the Indian home that they seldom lasted to become heirlooms. Today, the border pieces that lined *shamiana* (wedding tents) can be found and laid in contemporary rooms.

The low ceiling, the bug-bear of present day apartments, can be offset by these striking borders, which direct the eye downward and impose order, form, and effect on a plain room in much the same way as a painting can. The older dhurries, in stripes and bold colors, should not be overlooked in modern apartments for that simple stripe can visually widen or lengthen a room, a hallway or a narrow corridor.

Sisals and straws

Another floor covering indigenous to India, and well suited to country-style houses, is matting woven from coconut fibers. It comes in golden colors and has a good ribbed texture. Buy it in rolls and use a curved upholsterer's needle to stitch it together, or buy the English rush matting that looks so good in conservatories and country kitchens. American painter and fabric artist, Peter Fasano, gives a new look to classic sisal rugs using a water-based textile pigment rolled on in stripes. For heavy duty areas, he advises using acrylic or oil-based paints, perhaps creating a chevron pattern, on the textured background.

Wooden floors

The best background for rugs is a wooden floor. Over the last few years this style of exposed flooring has made a comeback everywhere — from the cheapest chipboard, stained a dark gray and sealed, to the intricate stenciling and painting that has captured the imagination of homeowners bored with uniformity. A new method of laying wooden floors has been devised: laying them on the diagonal to increase the feeling of space. British journalist, Maureen Walker has used this arrangement in her own house and she has encouraged the patina of age by waxing the floor rather than sealing it with polyurethane.

Rugs can anchor a room scheme, as in the fresh colors, clear background and abstract geometrics of the Indian dhurrie, a flat weave at one third the cost of Oriental rugs.

Armonie dhurries (**above**) from the Toulemonde Bochart collection are designed in France, woven in India. Coconut matting (**right**), sold by the meter from the same collection is heavy duty, rated suitable for use in kitchen/diners.

Original floor boards (**top, far right**), sanded and varnished are unadorned in this room.

Pale floor boards (**below, far right**) set off long, natural cotton curtains, both stenciled with a floral basket design. For the floor, three stencils were used: red for fruit, green for leaves, yellow for the basket. Either work with tube or tinned paints applied on a soft roller, fairly dry, or use spray paint as recommended by professional stenciler Lynn le Grice. Lay down the first stencil, mark its position and apply paint. When dry, repeat the process with the next stencil and at the end, when all the colors are dry, apply five coats of varnish. For the curtains, outline the stencil design with tailor's chalk and apply colors with fabric-dye felt pens or artists' acrylic paints.

There are four types of wooden flooring to choose from: strip flooring which comes in widths of 1½in to 3¾in (3.8 to 10cm) wide; wider planks which run from 3in (7.6cm) to 8in (20cm) wide; unit blocks which are square or rectangular pieces made up of short wood strips; and parquet which is a wood mosaic in square tiles.

Dark floorboards can be bleached and pickled to give a very pale, very smart appearance. Syrie Maugham, wife of Somerset Maugham and inventor of the all-white room in the 1920s, originated the bleached and pickled furniture look which caused Lady Mendl to comment 'One day darling Syrie will arrange to be pickled in her own coffin'. Water-based whitewash rubbed into the floorboards gives them an interesting bleached dapple, which is a smart background for a rug collection. Use a matt finish sealer to fix and preserve it. You can stain or darken floorboards without too much trouble, using a commercial stainer rubbed into boards that have been washed with decorators' soap. Five coats of polyurethane sealer will protect it and the boards can be cleaned with a solution of vinegar and water.

Another alternative is to paint floorboards with gloss paint. Use a dark color and cover it with colorful rugs, or use a bold color for a brighter effect. Clean the floor very thoroughly before you apply the paint.

Plain wooden boards can be given a stencil border, with the stencil repeated in the hemline of plain white or neutral curtains. You need three separate stencils, one for each color, which is why commercial packs are sold in sets of three. Take a bold design like fruit in a trellis basket, stick down the stencil and a border of newspaper to catch the spilt paint and paint the basket yellow. When the paint is dry, lift the stencil and place the second stencil over the design — for example, red for the fruit, green for the leaves and so on. Use special fabric paints for stenciling on fabric so that the curtains match the floorboards.

At Celanese House in New York, Michael Murdolo stenciled a giant climbing rose pattern on the floorboards, painted with a white matt finish base coat, then sealed it with polyurethane. With a mahogany four-poster bed with a canopy, ruffled drapes and counterpane in a rose printed fabric, the flowery room took on a summery country freshness (stenciling, see page 203). By contrast, the latest hand-painted wooden panels and linoleums which reproduce baroque and Palladian patterns for the home reflect a completely different mood. Panels of interlocking

Natural materials, such as stone, bricks or terrazzo can now be faked, since we live in an age of illusion. The wealth of design aimed to deceive includes these astonishing floor patterns reproduced on linoleum (**right and center**) and vinyl (**far right**).

Flooring patterns based on designs from Venetian churches, originally in marble and mosaic, are transferred to linoleum (**right**) once regarded as a rather dreary floor covering. This is the inspiration of designers Peter Sheppard and Keith Day. They also hand-marble floor panels in tongue-and-grooved sections, ½ inch (12mm) thick.

A design (**far right**) taken from the Basilica San Marco must be laid in a brickwork pattern to achieve the optical effect of a raised pattern. Palladio, a design which appears all over Western Europe from classical times until the present day, is found in Renaissance churches, eighteenth-century houses and town houses and is used now to great effect, in the Sheppard/Day house.

Hand-marble your own floors, taking baroque designs from churches and Italian terrazzo and the paving of piazzas. To hand-marble hardboard panels, rub down the surface with Lubrisil paper 165 and apply wood primer, an undercoat the same color as the top finish, before you apply three layers of eggshell paint. Sand down the surface when it is completely dry and be careful that the sanding does not cause ridging on your paint effect. Choose two or three paint colors to apply as veins over the eggshell coat, and mix them into scumble glaze, available from an artists' supplier. Try earth colors — raw umber, burnt sienna, yellow ocher. With a fine brush dipped into thinners, trace on veining in each color, dabbing and sweeping loosely. Draw the lines close and then apart, but never crossed to create sharp angles. Then take a stippling brush and stab at the lines buying crafted finishes by the yard or meter on cushion backed vinyls. This marble finishes, such as black with yellow ocher or olive greens and jade on brown.

tongue-and-groove boards, which measure about 2ft 60cm) square and ½in (13mm) thick, are hand-marbled with designs from Venetian churches. The designers Peter Sheppard and Keith Day have used the designs in their old rectory in Oxfordshire, England. The most baroque design, 'San Zaccaria', comes in a white marble finish, black portico and pink fossil stone, while the timeless 'Palladio' reproduces faithfully the white marbled squares, set with small diamonds in different colors — blue lapis, green onyx, pink fossil stone, black and sienna.

Tiling

In modern houses, tiles are no longer confined to the kitchen or the bathroom because central heating makes them a viable proposition in a living room. Consequently, designs have changed to include patterns in turquoise and terracotta copied from the floors of Turkish mosques. They are sold in packs of six to make up a panel every bit as elaborate as a Turkish carpet.

There are three types of ceramic tile available today: glazed tiles which are shiny and smooth, matt finish tiles (called monocottura in the USA) which come mainly in solid colors, and unglazed tiles in natural earth tones. Sizes for all these range from 1in (2.5cm) square to 1ft (30cm) square, including hexagonal and rectangular tiles.

Tiles make a practical floor covering under solid fuel or wood burning stoves that have a chimney flue attachment. In a studio with a raised platform to divide the sleeping area from the living area, the ceramic tiles can be extended in a diagonal line to the platform linking the areas.

Vinyls

Vinyl, the success story of the sixties, relegated in the snobbish seventies to second place, is now making a comeback in the smartest homes. Popular patterns are surprisingly traditional for such a space-age material. There are also some innovative vinyls, such as the brightly colored vinyl duckboard matting, or the

Man-made floor coverings range from glazed tiles to vinyl (**left**), a sturdy and practical base for the kitchen. The intricate design of chevron tiles, brickwork or herringbone pattern would take a tiler weeks to achieve, and then the flooring underfoot would be both hard and cold. Use fakes to expand your horizons on a large scale, to blur the edges of the veining. Try also contrasting color schemes for Amtico herringbone floor pattern reproduces the grand expanses of hand-laid tiles, and creates an orderly base to the modern kitchen, with its folding chairs, breakfast bar and double oven, and a trolley for speedy removal of clutter.

rubber stud industrial flooring, which architect Eva Jiricna uses in high-tech homes.

Vinyl, in sheet or tile form, can be laid over almost any surface without a problem. You can cover an entire floor with vinyl quarry tiles with the help of a sharp-edged decorator's knife and some adhesive for a quarter of the price and time it takes to lay a genuine quarry-tiled floor. Varying thicknesses of vinyl will produce stone, slate, parquet or brick effect. A popular vinyl is the black and white diamond flooring.

Cork and chipboard
Tiles in cork are less fun, but every bit as practical. They make a discreet dappled background in many a home and can also act as bulletin boards. Some cork tiles can be bought ready sealed, but others need a double coating of matt varnish. Chipboard squares from builders' stores can be stained to reproduce the color of almost any wood, but they are very porous so you must use plenty of stain and seal the squares very carefully.

White industrial flooring, a molded plastic chair and designer white laminate round table. chrome sculptures and four-panel abstract painting, plus a palm in a white box, is what architect Eva Jiriċna has teamed with other high-tech components in the look for which her interiors are known (**right**).

Amtico have a range of tongue-and-grooved mock floorboards (**below right**), shown here with a wooden sycamore bowl on a little wooden low table, so faithfully done that the eye is deceived.

Brick flooring (**below far right**) is cheap to buy and gives a warm, natural earthenware appeal.

The owners of this eighteenth-century house in Connecticut chose an Oriental rug they liked and gave it to artist John Canning to reproduce as a trompe l'oeil painting (**left**). John Canning, apprenticed in Glasgow as a church decorator, concentrated on stenciling for wall and floor decorations and cut stencils for the medallions and motifs of this painted rug, following the original colors of indigo, amber hunting green, plum, scarlet, black and cream.

LIGHTING

No design for a room is complete until it takes account of the shape and placing of light sources, the colour and mood of the light.

Lighting may not appear to be an obvious asset in the home, but it is a crucial ingredient in creating atmosphere. Without good lighting, even the most stylish room can become dull and characterless. Lighting is seldom considered to be a contributory factor in the success or failure of a room because our understanding of it is limited. Unfortunately the lighting in a room cannot be easily captured by photography — the medium through which most people learn about design.

When you decorate a room, be sure to consider the lighting. It may be too harsh, without any softness or play between light and shade, or it may be dim or yellowing. A few changes can rectify this. A recessed fixture in the ceiling, surfaces that indirectly reflect the light source (mirror tiles round the fireplace or window sill) or replacing conventional switches with dimmer switches could make all the difference. All you need to understand is how to control the level of light intensity and how to apply this to individual areas.

Concentrated light from lamps or fittings is needed to back up good general lighting from invisible sources like recessed downlights. Here are two examples of fittings selected to suit the period setting of the rooms, with mirrors to reflect their light.
This grouping of Victorian lamp shades in abalone shell, opaque glass and glass inset with a lacy panel, all fringed (**right**) and beaded, bestow charm and variety. Gentle pools of light are reflected in the diamond mirror inset in the bamboo wall-hanging, on which the silk kimono and collection of old glass scent bottles add to the unusual period style.
A contemporary setting in the Blumert residence in New York City (**center**) where the bold color scheme selected by designers Ohrbach/Jacobson is reflected in the mirrored wall. Spots on track show the undisguised practicality of track lighting, considered not just acceptable, but decorative.

Bold colors of emerald and purple in the Skelzo apartment (**above**) are illuminated by spots on tracks around the room. Designer Roger Bazeley screens the windows with horizontal Venitian blinds to let in as much natural light as possible, and sets a mirror as a bedhead to bounce back the light. The bedside lamps are the latest angular modern fittings, chosen to complement the contemporary design of this bedroom.

No curtains screen the rather narrow window in this kitchen/diner (**left**), but a pretty white frill set at valance level draws attention to the window and source of natural light. The overhead light above the dining table with its white cone shade is on a dimmer switch, essential for controlling the intensity of light and creating a soft atmosphere when required.

David Hersey, lighting designer for DHA Lighting Company, is recognized as Europe's leading lighting expert. He has lit operas, ballets, shows on Broadway and in London, as well as the triumphant 'Guys and Dolls' for the National Theatre in London where he was the lighting consultant for 10 years. He considers lighting to be the most unifying element in a production, capable of portraying the entire structure of a set. Sometimes this is an astonishing feat to execute. In the Lloyd-Weber/Price musical 'Starlight Express' actors travel on roller skates at 18 mph to give the effect of speeding trains. For this show David Hersey is required to light a suspension bridge 30ft (9m) wide with several hundred lumenaires. The bridge is hung 80ft (24m) in the air. He explains: 'The whole production is about movement and the light has to respond, so I have designed motorized spots, operated by computer to move with the action of the bridge and the choreography'.

Clearly modern technology has more to offer than the domestic electric bulb, hanging from a wire in the middle of a room. Yet David Hersey is far from dismissive about such conventional light fittings, using them in his own home but with variations. His advice to home-owners is to remove light switches and replace them with dimmer switches (like an adapter that controls the fittings). At the turn of a switch, a dimmer will vary the level of light. Dimmers save bulb life and reduce the electricity consumption. More importantly, they enable you to control the light so that you can create the atmosphere you want. Simple dimmers merely replace the usual light switch; the multiple control units handle several circuits from the same point.

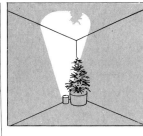

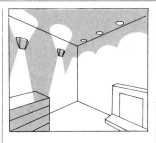

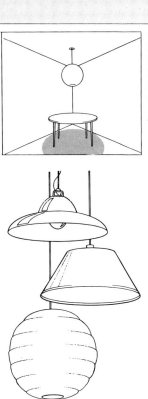

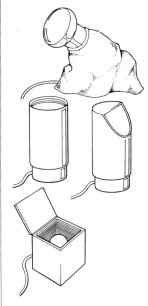

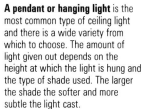

A pendant or hanging light is the most common type of ceiling light and there is a wide variety from which to choose. The amount of light given out depends on the height at which the light is hung and the type of shade used. The larger the shade the softer and more subtle the light cast.

Although pendant lights provide good general light, they tend to flatten shadows and they can also look obtrusive hanging from the ceiling. They are most useful over a table directing light downward. You can vary the amount of light given out by using a rise and fall fixture.

Uplights can be used very effectively with downlighters to give a good atmosphere to a room. Designed to be placed on the floor, they can be positioned in a variety of places. Try them behind plants or large pieces of furniture, beneath glass shelves or in corners. You will find that they produce 'accent' lighting that has a very dramatic effect on the room.

Downlights These are round or square metal cannisters recessed or semi-recessed into ceilings so that they cast pools of light onto the surface below. The bulb is either a spot or a floodlight. A spot will give a concentrated circle of light, while a floodlight will give a wider, less intense cone-shaped light. Most downlighters are fitted with an anti-glare device, such as a gold or silver reflector for directional light. Gold reflectors give a warm light, silver ones give a harsher light.

Downlights can also make color more brilliant and moldings more effective, but they need to be placed very carefully. Use downlights sparingly in the living room; table lamps are more suitable for an overall cosy glow. A domestic version of a theater floodlight has adjustable flaps top and bottom to shield the bulb. With the flaps open you can bathe a wall with light.

Three kinds of light-fitting are in one room (**above**): the table-lamp casting a pool of light downward, the pendant light above the dining table screened with the Italian woven straw fan shade, and the wall-mounted light, a tall fan, spreading the light to bathe the wall. Even the poster of Olympic water sports has a dancing, reflective quality of light in its broken water pattern. Furnishings are chosen in different textures that work together: shag-pile carpet, black leather sofa, white lacquer table and silk wallcovering. In designer Leila Corbett's room, a juxtaposition of lights at very different heights focuses attention around the bed.

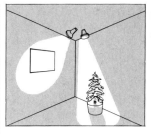

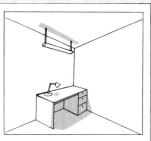

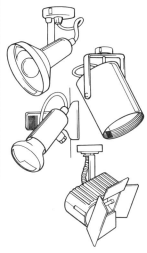

Spotlights and tracks Spots are usually mounted straight onto ceilings or walls or onto track systems. In this way they are used as 'accent' lighting to highlight particular objects. The simplest spot holds a reflector fitting for an ordinary bulb; a special spot bulb has an internal silvered reflector for intensity. The most expensive, and usually the bulkiest, has a low voltage transformer inside the spot that will cast a narrow beam onto small objects or specific areas.

Tracks are good for getting the maximum light from one outlet without incurring extra electrical work. Fix tracks across the middle of the ceiling, or down the wall for flexibility. You can cross light beams at steep angles in a high-ceilinged room so that you are not looking directly at a beam of light. Tracks allow for all kinds of lighting experimentation.

Freestanding Lamps Often it is better to have a number of small sources of light, rather than one main source, such as an overhead light. Keep a couple of points on every wall for general or directional light — from table or floor lamps. Adjustable table lamps provide useful directional light for reading. Floor lamps can be fitted with spotlights that act as a substitute for wall-mounted tracks. Lamp shades can be chosen to give off the amount of light you need, and they can be decorative in colored silk, paper or linen. Avoid using colored bulbs; alter intensity with the use of dimmer switches.

Desk lamps These are designed to provide concentrated areas of light and are essential for close work. They should be adjustable so that you can alter the fall of light. Desk lamps come in a variety of forms including clip-on lamps and high-tech style lamps.

For specific information on lighting for kitchens and bathrooms, see pages 178 and 202.

STYLE

Style: most sought after; most difficult to pin down. You may know someone who possesses that indefinable quality, just as you recognize it in a room or a house. Never confuse style with character. Property agents' endorsements of character — inglenook fireplaces and a collection of horse brasses — carry no pretence of style. Yet humble materials in the same setting — a drag washed apricot wall, rush matting underfoot, a basket for logs, loose covers in a flowery print on a comfortable sofa and basket chairs in all the colors of a pot-pourri — could be stylish.

Style has little to do with good taste either. The apartment of French designer, Olivier Gagnère, could hardly be described as tasteful, yet his bedroom is stylish in a most unusual way. He uses an invalid's steel walking frame as a clothes rack, keeps his television on a skateboard and installs his telephone on an extendable trellised arm at his bedside. As a backdrop for this mobile furnishing he chooses white lacquered walls, white painted floorboards and black Venetian blinds. It is this sense of drama, coupled with a deft use of materials, that creates his particular brand of style.

Stylish interiors constantly change, absorbing new enthusiasms in a timeless setting: pictures are moved about, patterns are transposed, a piece of glass suggests the color of a piece of silk, a collection builds up on a tabletop, and a lamp highlights some new find.

Professional stylists who create live-in interiors, rather than those artificial room-sets for magazines, are loosely grouped as designer/architects, and

interior decorators. The designer will consider the structure of the interior, make the most of space and light and add architectural details if necessary. The decorator chooses the materials and furniture to fit the scheme. Style is ageless: Art Deco stainless steel, chrome and black lacquer is used in an open-plan apartment; high-backed dark wood bedhead, chairs, towel rack and shoe rack sit in a Shaker-inspired, white-washed bedroom of monastic simplicity in New York City; Bauhaus geometrics are reproduced on Liberty cotton for 1980s upholstery, or car paint is sprayed on industrial components to complement the interiors of London architect, Eva Jiricna. All these contemporary interiors and furnishings have an originality that is timeless.

Modern interior design styles are numerous, so in order to provide guidelines for choosing one, this section covers the four major themes. They are grand style, which has its roots in the past, borrowing freely from classicism to Vic-

Today's interiors are different from those of a decade ago. If you go further back most styles are classified as retro (which is stylish anyway). Yet there is a timelessness about good style which pervades in every case. Call it a sense of scale, proportion, color, individualism, even a sense of humor. Here are two examples of style, very different in the statement they make about the people who live in them. The first uses pattern upon pattern in a room designed by printmaker and painter Howard Hodgkin (**left**). Even the table has an inky imprint that makes it more charming. Howard Hodgkin believes that rooms are self-expressions so he ignores the angst-ridden attention to period detail of many interior designers. His fabrics, furniture and lamps were designed for the British Arts Council 'Four Rooms' exhibition of 1984.

Piers Gough's renovated warehouse in London's East End (**right**) is stylish. The window drapes of Bolton sheeting echo the shape of the wheat-sheaf table base. Style is an individual thing, and while you may not like a particular style, it is useful to be able to identify it. There are the curves of the tubular chrome chairs and the rounded table top, the vertical slats of the window against the horizontal line-up of floorboards, the tub lilies set at the same height on either side of the window with a true regard for symmetry. If you consider the components of the room, they amount to no more than the simplest of drapes, two pictures, two flowers, and three items of furniture. Yet the proportions of the room, the natural sense of form and balance, are fully exploited.

A witty interpretation of function and purpose is revealed in Marc Chaimowicz's desk and filing cabinet designed for the 'Four Rooms' exhibition (**above**). The 'lying-down' desk symbolizes the artist's difficulty with the written word, yet there is real practicality in the filing cabinet design — a column to fill a space. Chaimowicz sees the interior as an ideal room to do nothing in. And there is a contemplative restfulness about the soft blues, the wavy lines of his fabrics, and the colored glass panel set high in the wall.

The loft apartment of Ger van Elk in Amsterdam (**right**) displays the owner's love for Art Deco. His few handsome pieces are set against a spacious, restrained background. Notice how the furniture and lamp are anchored by the rug, and only the two handsome tables break out of its confines to become display pieces on the golden floorboards.

toriana; the country house style that combines simple crafts with down-to-earth materials; modernism which includes post-modernism, minimalism and high-tech; and eclectic — those idiosyncratic styles, such as surrealist, kitsch and retro, that defy conventional grouping.

Inspiration for style

Everyone has a particular room, or style of room, that they like or feel comfortable in. Inspiration for details often come from unexpected sources, so always take notes when you respond favorably to an interior. Designers and decorators do this all the time, scribbling down such details as picture framing, colors, lamp shades, and wall finishes.

So a lifesize sepia photograph of Charles Darwin's study, used as a backdrop in an exhibition at the Science Museum in London, produces some interesting design ideas based on Victoriana. The workmanlike scene, featuring bookshelves on either side of the fireplace, screened by a small curtain on rails, and the marble mantelpiece surround with a still-life of nature studies suggest the bookish and studious atmosphere suitable for a library or study

room. By contrast, a recent exhibition of the work of Raoul Dufy acted as inspiration for a range of fabrics, based on 1920s designs, showing willow and wheat-sheaf patterns in primary colors on a gigantic scale. Sometimes the work of a designer disappears for a generation and is then rediscovered and restored, or copied in a different setting at a later date. In 1980 the 'Willow' tearooms in Glasgow, Scotland, were renovated using the original designs for furnishings (lamps, rugs, even cutlery) of Scottish-born architect Charles Rennie Mackintosh (1868-1928). The single peacock feather motif and the tall ladderback chairs — both features of his interiors — were used in the decor.

In the twenties, Irish designer Eileen Gray combined the thoroughness of the Bauhaus tradition with an oriental exoticism, for the interior of her house in Roquebrune, France. She used an interesting juxtaposition of steel, sycamore and glass, padded leather and lacquer for the closets and cabinets, furniture and furnishings, mirrors and light fittings.

Alternatively, it may be from paintings that we get inspiration for interior decorating: those cosy domestic scenes of Edouard Vuillard's, for example, in soft pinks, grays and lilacs, or Claude Monet's home at Giverny with the rush chairs in two tones of yellow, the blue and white china, and the terracotta tiles. Van Gogh's bedroom at Arles, simply furnished, yet brightly colored in sunshine yellow and blue, provides a basis for a stylish decorative scheme. Notice how the colors in these paintings always contrast light and dark, pale and deep. The current enthusiasm for pastels in formless rooms — icecream colors that threaten to melt away — merely emphasizes this point.

Interior designer Diana Phipps always adds a smidgeon of black to her color schemes, off-setting the yellow and white gingham in her bedroom, for example. She uses black canopy supports, or threads a black velvet ribbon through an eyelet bed pillowcase. Colefax and Fowler introduced a striking citric lemon to cut through the softness of pretty pastels in their newest Brook collection of chintzes. Even the minimalists, whose interiors are devoid of positive statements, so that paintings are propped against the wall and seldom hung lest they give an air of permanence to a place, will use a sharp color on a cornice or baseboard to anchor the neutrals.

Contemporary rooms in houses built after World War II, reflect their time in many different ways. The height of the rooms, for example, suits the

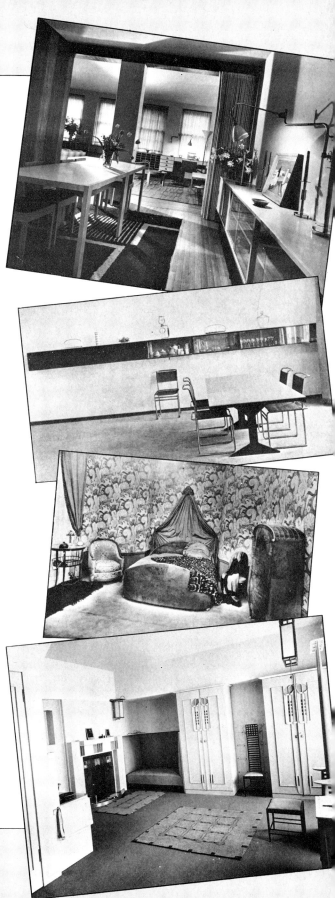

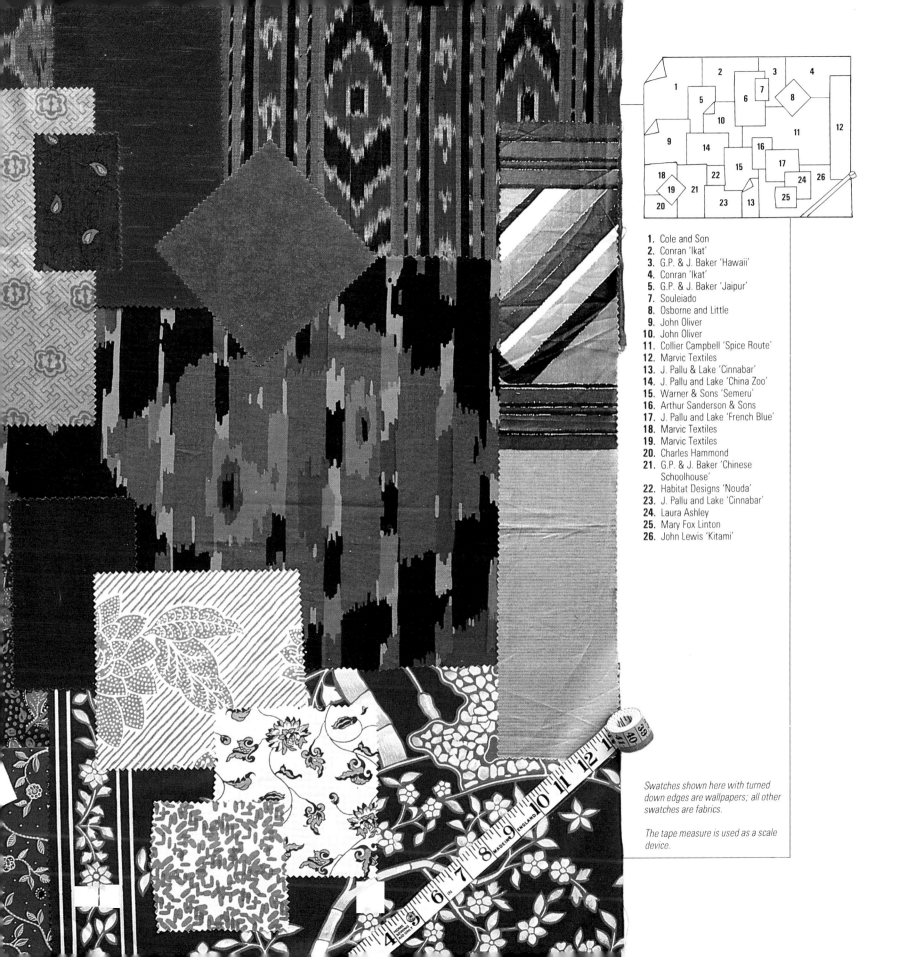

1. Cole and Son
2. Conran 'Ikat'
3. G.P. & J. Baker 'Hawaii'
4. Conran 'Ikat'
5. G.P. & J. Baker 'Jaipur'
7. Souleiado
8. Osborne and Little
9. John Oliver
10. John Oliver
11. Collier Campbell 'Spice Route'
12. Marvic Textiles
13. J. Pallu & Lake 'Cinnabar'
14. J. Pallu and Lake 'China Zoo'
15. Warner & Sons 'Semeru'
16. Arthur Sanderson & Sons
17. J. Pallu and Lake 'French Blue'
18. Marvic Textiles
19. Marvic Textiles
20. Charles Hammond
21. G.P. & J. Baker 'Chinese Schoolhouse'
22. Habitat Designs 'Nouda'
23. J. Pallu and Lake 'Cinnabar'
24. Laura Ashley
25. Mary Fox Linton
26. John Lewis 'Kitami'

Swatches shown here with turned down edges are wallpapers; all other swatches are fabrics.

The tape measure is used as a scale device.

The document colors

Archive prints that are still popularly printed by the big textile designers usually have documented colors accompanying them. These specify that the leaves, if any, will be blue. This dates back to the time when vegetable dyes were used and yellow was overprinted on blue to get the green on leaves. The yellow always faded. Today's blue leaf comes from synthetic dyes but the presence of it means a document color. Often hand-blocked prints form the collection on backgrounds the shade of pale tea. Some manufacturers still use the original pear wood blocks, now 120 years old.

In the nineteenth century, William Morris gave this advice 'Have nothing in your house that you do not know to be useful or believe to be beautiful.' Today his patterns are documented. The designs of Owen Jones, a Victorian interior designer are also influential today. Mostly these designs are large, for Victorian buildings were more generously proportioned, but some have been scaled down for contemporary living, and there exists today a line of wallpaper and upholstery fabric with a Gothic pattern and navy, burgundy and coloring that has been named 'Mr Jones'.

1. Cole and Son
2. Lee/Jofa
3. Tissunique 'Thorpe Hall'
4. G.P. & J. Baker 'Hungarian Point'
5. Liberty 'Honeysuckle'
6. Laura Ashley
7. Laura Ashley
8. G.P. & J. Baker 'Beauchamp'
9. Colefax and Fowler 'Haseley Acorn'
10. Arthur Sanderson and Sons 'Seaweed'
11. Chalon 'Forest Green' from Tissunique
12. Liberty 'Sita'
13. Laura Ashley
14. Laura Ashley
15. Arthur Sanderson & Sons 'Art Nouveau'
16. Liberty 'Hera'
17. Arthur Sanderson & Sons
18. John Oliver
19. Colefax and Fowler 'Passion Flower'
20. John Oliver

Swatches shown here with turned down edges are wallpapers; all other swatches are fabrics.

The tape measure is used as a scale device.

The neutrals

Coloring with neutrals is a matter of balancing the textures on floors and walls, with soft furnishings to off-set one against the other. It needs skill; a dash of magenta or a hint of ice blue can warm up or cool down the scheme and sharpen the mixture. Too much, and you will flatten them. Neutrals can be creamy with the brown tones, or icy with the blue greys. In India the five shades of white are actually specified in the ancient Vedic texts as the white of ivory, jasmine, sandalwood, moon-white (blued) and water-white (reflective).

In her New Delhi home, Pupul Jayakar, India's cultural director and organizer of the Festival of India worldwide has sandalwood tables set upon pale rush matting, walls painted in water-white to reflect a collection of paintings and form a backdrop to her art treasures of ancient stone carvings, terracotta figures, a bronze water vessel from Gujarat. 'In India we are known for our brilliant colors,' she says. 'Saffron, indigo, turmeric and chili red. Yet our skill in decorating lies in the harmony of tone, balance and texture in all the shades of white.

Neutrals are flexible and easy to revive when you tire of a season's color. Pep up last year's white and cream with bright accessories, a fresh plant, some contrast color on the baseboards or piping round the sofa cushions.

Sir Cecil Beaton wrote of the 1920's passion for all-white rooms: 'The white world made fashionable in the interior decorations of Syrie Maugham invaded the photographic studios. Every texture of white was sought in order to give vitality and interest: fiberglass, sheets of gelatine, cutlet frills, coils of carnival paper streamers, doves, egg boxes, cardboard plates, plaster carvings, driftwood branches.'

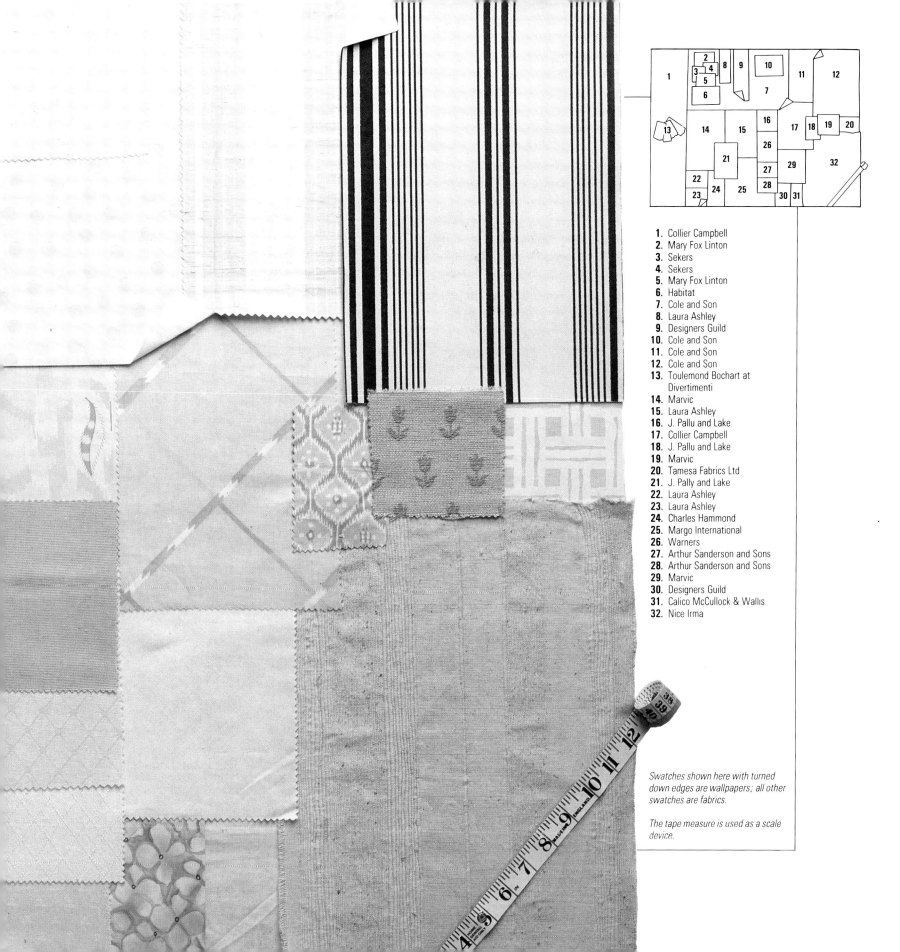

1. Collier Campbell
2. Mary Fox Linton
3. Sekers
4. Sekers
5. Mary Fox Linton
6. Habitat
7. Cole and Son
8. Laura Ashley
9. Designers Guild
10. Cole and Son
11. Cole and Son
12. Cole and Son
13. Toulemond Bochart at Divertimenti
14. Marvic
15. Laura Ashley
16. J. Pallu and Lake
17. Collier Campbell
18. J. Pallu and Lake
19. Marvic
20. Tamesa Fabrics Ltd
21. J. Pally and Lake
22. Laura Ashley
23. Laura Ashley
24. Charles Hammond
25. Margo International
26. Warners
27. Arthur Sanderson and Sons
28. Arthur Sanderson and Sons
29. Marvic
30. Designers Guild
31. Calico McCullock & Wallis
32. Nice Irma

Swatches shown here with turned down edges are wallpapers; all other swatches are fabrics.

The tape measure is used as a scale device.

Allied to the white look and the neutrals is the pale palette. This is the look of the faded chintzes, the soft colors of old rugs, pot pourri and summer gardens, the sort of look that has come to represent English style. Yet this country-house look translates well to the urban interiors in the icecream and candy colors of ice blue, soft pink, pale yellow, mint green and lavender. Pastels are mostly used round the room in multicolor combinations accented with deeper or sharper shades. To her 'Watercolor' collection, Tricia Guild of Designer's Guild adds a touch of deepest magenta to the softest colorings, as a piping on the sofa.

The pastels can be muddied a little the way painter Edouard Vuillard saw them in his interiors, with old rose and gray-blue accented with ocher and gray or charcoal.

1. Colefax and Fowler
2. J. Pallu and Lake Furnishings 'Canary'
3. G.P. & J. Baker 'Sierra'
4. G.P. & J. Baker 'Solange'
5. Marvic Textiles
6. Mary Fox Linton
7. Mary Fox Linton
8. J. Pallu and Lake Furnishings
9. Sekers Fabrics 'Brampton'
10. Liberty 'Sweetpea'
11. Toulemond Bochart at Divertimenti
12. Collier Campbell 'Raffia Braid'
13. Collier Campbell 'Okra'
14. Osborne and Little
15. J. Pallu and Lake Furnishings 'Surabaya'
16. J. Pallu and Lake Furnishings
17. Habitat
18. Tissunique
19. Warner & Sons 'Wood Anemone'
20. Marvic Textiles 'Seersucker'
21. Designers Guild
22. Designers Guild
23. Designers Guild
24. Designers Guild
25. Sekers Fabrics 'Arkley'
26. Osborne and Little 'Messara'
27. J. Pallu and Lake Furnishings 'Primrose'
28. J. Pallu and Lake Furnishings

Swatches shown here with turned down edges are wallpapers; all other swatches are fabrics.

The tape measure is used as a scale device.

The mediterranean colors

Colors that dance with light, with the blue of the sea, the sky, the jade of the Greek-island sea, the sunny yellows and bleached sands of summer.

Use white for contrast, for coolness, or add the dusty green of olives, and terracotta and melon shades to hold down those vibrant blues. If the fabrics carry the pattern and color, accent the upholstery.

Use jute matting or white tiles underfoot, paint open brickwork white, add basket-weaves and terracotta pots with plants. Patterns in this range seem to dance with light in the irregular wavy lines of birds on the wing, palm fronds that move, sandy ripples and dancing waves. Reduce their intensity with shade, damping down with the pales and the charcoals.

1. Collier Campbell 'Cote d'Azure'
2. Designers Guild papers and fabrics
3. Jonelle 'Bergen'
4. Mary Fox Linton 'Blue Waves'
5. Nice Irma's
6. Tamesa Fabrics
7. Tissunique 'Bleu Ciel'
8. Tissunique 'Poussin'
9. Desingers Guild 'Moonshine'
10. Warners & Sons 'Parasol Stripe'
11. Margo International
12. G.P. & J. Baker 'Sierra'
13. G.P. & J. Baker 'Sierra'
14. Habitat 'Pollen Ribbon'
15. Laura Ashley paper border
16. MacCulloch and Wallis ginghams
17. Laura Ashley 'Trellis'
18. J. Pallu and Lake Furnishings 'China Stripe'
19. Laura Ashley
20. J. Pallu and Lake Furnishings 'Nara'
21. J. Pallu and Lake Furnishings 'Trellis'
22. Arthur Sanderson & Sons
23. G.P. and J. Baker 'Lemon'
24. G.P. and J. Baker 'Ice Blue'
25. G.P. and J. Baker 'Mink'
26. G.P. and J. Baker 'Pistachio'

Swatches shown here with turned down edges are wallpapers; all other swatches are fabrics.

The tape measure is used as a scale device.

SECTION TWO

LIVING AREAS
MEDIA ROOMS AND WORK AREAS
BEDROOMS
KITCHENS
BATHROOMS
AWKWARD SPACES

LIVING AREAS

At the time of unpacking crates after a move, priorities vary in every household, but the living room is usually the first area to receive attention. Few people begin from scratch with no belongings or furniture and it is important to evaluate what you have before you plan the layout of the room.

For some people it is essential to get the sound system working; consideration is given to positioning speakers for the best acoustics, or placing the television where it will get the best reception and be easily accessible for the video and home computer. For others it is the china collection that needs to be displayed, graphics that require lighting, or books that must be cleared from vital floor space and put away in the correct place. Seldom will a library fit into self-assembly storage units and a quantity of larger books cannot be displayed on a single coffee table.

Throughout the house our enthusiasms determine the style of each room. The minimalist, who dislikes clutter, will be preoccupied with the business of storing things behind blinds, or in trunks, and letting the bedding roll serve as a backrest on platform seating by day, to be unfolded on a sleeping mat at night. The traditionalist will be busy stapling lengths of fabric to the walls to match patterns, pasting up a wallpaper border to coordinate with paint colors, and dressing the windows. Country lovers in urban dwellings will concentrate on stripping pine furniture, dabbing color onto mantelpieces and cutting stencils for floorboards.

Assess your living area carefully before you go out and buy metres of expensive fabric or choose wall colours. Consider such questions as who will be using the room, and for what purpose. How much natural daylight does the room have? Study the light and shadow for days before deciding whether it is a bright, average or dull room. North-facing rooms are generally too chilly for blues, for example, unless you choose a bold, bright blue, warmed up with amber; this looks cosy with night lighting.

What kind of lighting is there in the room? You may want to replace ordinary light switches with dimmer circuits so that you will have more control over the intensity of light. Fitting semi-recessed downlighters in the ceiling with low voltage beams can wash the walls with an effective light, but this is not a job for an amateur; for anything complicated, you should consult a lighting expert. Low voltage lights need either a built-in transformer or a separate transformer that can be recessed in the ceiling. A lighting consultant will give you a light show to demonstrate how effectively lighting creates the right atmosphere in a room. Reflectors on spot bulbs can bathe a room in a friendly golden light; a silvery reflector can

Seating arrangements are most important in your living room. Alternatives to the traditional furniture like the Chesterfield button-back, or the ubiquitous three-piece of contemporary living, are offered in these two living rooms. Painted and upholstered, occasional chairs can become a decorative asset in a room.
A junk-shop armchair (**left**) is given a slip cover of Collier Campbell's 'Rafia Rose' in tapestry colors from their American Chintz collection, the cushion is covered in 'Okra', the wall in Rafia Braid. The irregular stripes of the wall fabric are suited to the quick method of fabric wall-covering: using spray mount to glue directly onto the wall. Plainer fabrics stapled to the wall over a padded backing will give another effect (see page 136).
A Lloyd Loom chair in duck-egg blue (**right**) anchors the pastel color scheme in journalist Maureen Walker's living room.
To combine the living and dining room, builders knocked down the dividing wall, fitted a reinforced steel joist, and replaced the standard window at the far end to give more daylight. The background is understated: the curtains are made from lining fabric tied on a pole with sewing tape, the flooring is pale wood, waxed rather than varnished to a gentle golden patina and laid diagonally to give the illusion of space extending to the wall. There is an individual collection of old and new objects in the room: the ornate mirror was a bargain buy, the 'Tizzio' lamp is a Richard Sapper design for Italian Artemide.

This old apartment with chronic damp was converted into this airy living room with its attic bedroom (**above**). Advice from architect friends who had lived in Japan clearly influenced the decor of low seating and restrained colors. Furniture is kept to a minimum so she can move things around to change the look. She prefers to sit on the floor than in a chair, hence her low-level seating with bolstered sofa. Walls are painted soft gray, the Indian flat-weave dhurrie rug is in the pastel colors she favors. Thinned gray paint has been painstakingly rubbed into the grain of the floorboards to silver them before sealing with varnish.

make it more mysterious. Filters can be used to create moonlight effects, or make conservatories seem more lush; spots or projectors can specifically light shelves and paintings while downlights and uplights flood a wall with light. Once you have learned how to control lighting, you can create interesting shadow patterns by filtering light through the leaves of a plant or behind a piece of coral.

Next, work out what surfaces you will repaint or cover. These will include floors, ceilings, walls, cornices and baseboards, doors and frames, radiators and windows as well as shelving. Take into consideration the kind of house you live in. Is it semi-detached, ranch style, an apartment, or a period residence'? The dimensions of the room — its length, width and height — could influence your choice of color as much as the style of furnishing. Architect John Pawlson

chose to create a minimalist interior in a mid-Victorian house, but retained the original cornices, and painted the moldings a startling pink. This is one way of using architectural detail without letting it dominate the room. Often the grace and beauty of a period building dictates its own decoration. In a small box house the choice is greater and almost anything you do will improve it. A simple color throughout will widen horizons, but make sure the wall finish is good. Pay particular attention to color in details, such as door trims and handles, electrical sockets and window frames, all of which can all benefit from a contrasting color.

List the colors you like or dislike. Dark blue may remind you of a uniform, but a similar color, called indigo and peppered with saffron and paprika, may suggest something more exotic. Response to color is a very individual thing and adjectives used by manufacturers to sell their products, such as 'restful', 'vibrant' or 'exotic' will not make you like better those you react against. Instead use adjectives to describe the mood or effect you want to create — spacious or cosy, dramatic or restrained, warm or cool, restful or exciting. Some paint manufacturers sell tiny sample pots of paint so that you can try the effect in your own living room.

Barratt, the biggest house-builders in Britain, made a positive statement about lifestyle in the 1980s when they launched a scheme of apartments for the new generation of house buyers. Despite the stolid name of 'The Dorchester Suite', there is little that is traditional about the concept, either in the floor plans or the decoration of the rooms. The 'Harmony' interior is designed for two singles jointly purchasing an apartment, and it contains two bedrooms, each with a bathroom and dressing room en suite; 'Tempo' is a studio for a single person, with one bathroom recessed from the living area and 'Accord' is a studio apartment for two with a double bedroom.

The designer, Margaret Byrne, chose furnishings for the three schemes that would reflect the different lifestyles of each. The black, gray and white color scheme of 'Harmony' gives the shared living areas a distinctive unity while allowing an individual color preference for accessories (she chose red). In the 'Tempo' interior the designer has struck out more boldly with an individual treatment of navy, red and white, using red gloss baseboards throughout to accent the navy carpet, and white piping on the nautical navy sofa. 'Accord' is more subtle, with pastel colors for furnishings, and gray lacquer fur-

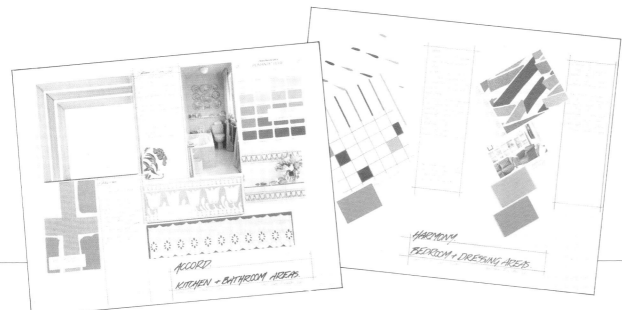

ACCORD.
KITCHEN + BATHROOM AREAS.

HARMONY
BEDROOM + DRESSING AREAS.

Pages from designer Margaret Byrne's notebook (**left**) illustrate how she drew up schemes for the Barratt's show houses at the 1984 Ideal Home exhibition in London. The dining/living room in the Accord one-bedroomed apartment (**above**) is unified by the color scheme. In the pages from her notebook, you can see how Margaret Byrne builds up color schemes around border patterns, paint color and fabric swatches. For your own scheme, pick out a multicolored fabric you would like to use in the living room for upholstery or curtains and isolate the colors for the walls, ceilings and floors. Then introduce accent colors that you recognize in the fabric design.

Hand-painted finishes can transform a fireplace surround or an architrave, turning such unlikely material into the focal point of the room (**above**).
John Canning's feathery strokes with a fine brush apply veining in a darker paint color mixed with scumble glaze on top of the eggshell base, to give a hand-marbled finish to this early American fireplace surround (**left**).

Tortoiseshelling the architrave on doors of differing heights draws attention to them (**above**), and the group of pictures hung on the yellow walls gives this potentially awkward corridor area of the living room a grand entrance.

niture set against the natural background tones of wood, cork and tinted glass to anchor the pales. Margaret Byrne's working notebook (page 99) shows how an interior decorator tackles a scheme from scratch.

Flooring covers the largest area in the room, so never underestimate how important it is to get it right. A brown carpet inherited in a dull apartment can deaden the entire scheme. Silky straw blinds, called chick in India, give the flooring throughout the same apartment a distinctive texture if laid directly onto the brown carpet. The material itself suggests a few instant decorating ideas — a large wicker tray with shells on it and paper fan shades.

Fabrics on the wall, or pinned to the window, will also give you an idea of the colors you can live with. Invest in a staple gun — the most powerful you can operate — and you can cover a wall temporarily with patterned double sheets. Put up poles above windows for simple drapes, or place simple shades in the window frames. Use narrow doweling cut to the right length and pinned to plasterwork with map indicator pins. This will be strong enough to hold a length of lace, a swatch of muslin, even an Indian sari in flimsy cheesecloth, knotted in one corner and swagged in loops over the pole. These may only be temporary measures but they will help you to define your style.

This living room (**left**) has a distinctive display of ducks on the walls, not the winged variety that classify kitsch today, but a handsome collection of decoys. They make a graceful setting for the upholstered green sofa. Rough plasterwork here enhances the sense of outdoors, so cleverly introduced with the solid greeen sofa and the dried grasses and flowers that seem part of the ducks' natural habitat. The white floor increases the sense of space in this narrow room as do the spotlights on curved aluminum tracks, freeing the floorspace of table or standard lamps, and illuminating the painting. Collections require a setting where they not only look at home, but can be enjoyed against a low-key background.

Finding a focus

Your living room is an introduction to your home. It is the room that people will be invited into most often. Those fortunate enough to have a fireplace will probably make it the focus of the room, around which chairs and sofa can be grouped. Undistinguished fireplaces can be enlivened with hand marbling; paint the surrounds with a mid-sheen base, then streak on artist's oils, mixed with gloss paint, in marbled shades of gray mixed with umber to darken it, or white to lighten it (see marbling page 23).

Prop a plain mirror above the mantelshelf to reflect the light from the opposite window into the room, and adorn it with a length of fabric draped across the top. Casually tie the fabric in the center, and at the top left and right corners with silk ribbons. Let the sides tumble down in swags on either side to hide the ugly mirror edges — an idea taken from the Laura Ashley decorators' showroom in London. Place a plaster bust or a porcelain bowl in front of it, with some lacquered boxes or silver frames to give a gracious double image.

In place of a mirror, you could hang a picture. Reproductions of old paintings in the right frame can look charming, as decorator Daphne Graham displayed when she put a print of Van Gogh's camellias in an ornately carved wooden frame that she had

More displays are illustrated here — this time using the traditional sideboard in unconventional forms. Ducks on the wall are set in a humorous application against the blue wall with the cloudlike backdrop of the purpose-built furniture (**above**). The lines of the sideboard are geometrically balanced with its angular base following the line of the curved top, an Art Deco device that is followed in the English Odeon cinema fronts of the 1930s. Theatrical, amusing, not grand, this showpiece is a talking point.

Restoring furniture can be satisfying and rewarding, but it does involve painstaking work. The most important step is the first one — to properly prepare the surface to be painted or varnished. The old finish should be removed carefully so that you get back to clean, bare wood. Any cracks or scars should be filled to provide an even surface.

The sideboard (**right**) was originally covered with black paint. This was carefully stripped off and the piece was covered with a gloss polyurethane varnish. The result (**far right**) is both pleasing and elegant.

scumbled with white and gray and rubbed down with steel wool to antique it. Make a note of the way pictures are framed so that you can create your own little gallery. A simple engraving, bought as a loose leaf in a book store, will look splendid on a gray mount with a beveled edge. A fine red line painted about a fingertip away from the beveled edge adds the perfect finishing touch. Put this in a red wooden or light-weight aluminum frame.

Furniture

In the living room it is often the furniture that is the focal point of the room, but just as in a garden, careful pruning is needed to bring out the best in a room. It can be an herbaceous border of pattern and color, the sort of charming picture that the Continental calls English style — but this requires careful consideration of both scale and proportion.

In a small, cramped room a large unit can house your stereo and television more effectively than a series of small tables. When you have decided on a theme, pick one really fine piece of upholstery to anchor it. Chipboard units and knockdown chairs never really improve with age — in fact they worsen — whereas a soft leather chair or good wood ages very well.

Slipcovers create an instant effect with upholstery. Hallie Greer, whose flourishing fabric business, 'Laurie Morrow', is called the 'Laura Ashley' of America, says: 'Slipcovers are practical as well as celebratory. They last twice as long as upholstery and transform the mood . . . the season's change is heralded by changing the slipcovers to cooler, more sprightly colors.'

If you don't want to use slipcovers, consider hanging 'throws' — a woven blanket, a Kashmiri shawl, or a piece of old patchwork — over the back of a sofa or chair. Never underestimate the value of plenty of cushions, with raw silk patterned embroidery covers, or home-made petit point from a tapestry kit. In a modern household, you could scatter these cushions on the floor, around low tables, and on platforms that are used for eating and seating.

One-room living

Whether you call the space a studio or a pied-à-terre, the one-room apartments of the inner cities are, ironically, the biggest growth area in twentieth-century housing. Entirely a product of the squeeze on inner-city space, these one-room apartments that perform as sleeping, sitting, working, and

Architect Piers Gough's room (**above**) shows the same sense of form in the balanced juxtaposition of an original designer's plan chest with its idiosyncratic collection of china dishes that take the form of the contents they were intended to house — a celery stalk jug, asparagus bunch dish, a bulbous fish for the soup tureen, vegetable and fruit bowls shaped like tomatoes and grapes respectively. Balance and symmetry inform this display with the added jolt of illumination of the peeling wall surfaces and damp.

The proportions of a room can be altered visually with different wall treatments that extend or shorten the run. Clever use of colors, fabrics, papers and furnishing, pictures and distractions can complement the scheme. What you do with a room's background is important because the areas involved on floors, walls, and ceilings are so large. Three ingenious solutions to create impeccable backgrounds are shown here, each using different wall treatments: rough plaster in an all-white room, a documented chintz used to line the walls and curtain the window in a modern townhouse, and a bold display of pictures and masks to occupy an entire wall. The rough plaster finish is painted white (**right**) and all the furnishing kept white to create a room of Mediterranean freshness and light, despite its tiny window. Space beneath the window is cleverly used to house shelves and an upholstered white sofa.

The rooms (**left**) show pattern on the walls in two variations, one created with fabric on the walls, the other with a collage of decorative pieces and pictures.

Interior designer David Mlinaric selected and colored designs found in old country houses for his National Trust collection made by Tissunique of Lyons. Erdigg, reproduced here in a chintz, was found in a late seventeenth-century house in North Wales, hidden under many layers on a fine set of chairs. Original fragments did not constitute a full repeat so the design has been completed in the same style and used here in a library (**above left**) in a modern town house in Blackheath, South London.

Owner/designer Gil Barber is an American model, actor and agent who collects American sheet music the theater posters. Each room is treated differently: this one (**bottom left**) is covered in pictures and masks from Bali which Gil rearranges frequently. Junk shop furniture is Gil's other enthusiasm. Her modern electronics and video are housed in an old sideboard. England of the 1930s and 1940s captures Gil's imagination, hence the 1930s standard lamp and Art Nouveau lamp from Milan. The art of hanging pictures together in well-planned groups is illustrated in this view — large Indian painting on cloth with vegetable dyes anchors one end and is hung at exactly the same height as the window at the far end of the collection; smaller pieces are hung near the window to benefit from the light, as the windows are kept bare.

Studios, the result of the urban squeeze on space, can be handled imaginatively as illustrated by these pictures of architects' apartments, one in Holland (**right**) and one in Britain (**far right**). Space can be divided, either structurally with platforms or with innovative furnishings, to make rooms twice as habitable.

High ceilings in this Amsterdam flat at Prinzengracht (**right**) meant that the architect owner could suspend his bed on a platform above the living area. So the bookshelves reach astonishing heights, yet books are at arm's length, depending on the level. Soft colors — a pink alcove, gray and white bed linen and the cream flooring — keep the room looking spacious.

cooking areas, demand a pragmatic treatment.

Architects tackle this problem with structural changes, sweeping away partition walls, removing parts of the ceiling, taking out doors to create a space that highlights the austerity of the structure. They will then go on to define the different areas with pits or platforms, panels of white muslin, simple white paper blinds or PVC roller blinds, or the slatted Venetian blinds that have replaced conventional walls to give slight, but significant divisions between areas.

Designers will favor furniture that folds up or folds out to create floor space, like the Murphy bed in America, or the sofa bed, as well as room divider shelving systems that mark off areas within a room and offer valuable storage space.

Both architects and designers will ensure that when space is at a premium, no section of the whole is totally divorced from the rest. American minimalist Joe d'Urso believes that functional items like bath furnishings should be on display too. From one end of the living room that he designed in the famous nineteenth-century Dakota building in New York, the pedestal basin is clearly visible. A sheet of glass screens the shower and lavatory, a half-height partition divides the kitchen and dining areas, and the space behind the stairs that lead to a platform bed is used as a seating area.

One-room living has inspired a whole range of furniture designed specifically to save space. This new approach brought about the demise of the matching three-piece suite, impossible to fit into irregular schemes and gave rise to modular push-together seats and ottomans that give smaller rooms new dimensions. Heavy, space-swallowing furniture is usually replaced by a small-scale, portable sofa that converts into a bed at night; tables that double up as desks and filing cabinets that serve as bedside tables. Spotlight systems can be set into tracks across walls and ceilings, which frees floor space from standard lamps. Even fittings are adaptable, even mobile, in these new schemes. Clip-on shelving, also on tracks, can be adjusted to house various sizes of books and objects.

Anything on wheels — from vacuum cleaners and filing cabinets to clothes racks and TV trolleys — can be contemporary solutions to restricted space, while hooks on the walls, traditionally used as pegs, can support tabletops, folding chairs, even beds.

Architects Christopher Williamson and Karen Moloney hook their six-foot-square mattress on to the wall and cover it in a lightweight nylon kite material that makes it an abstract wall-hanging by day in their

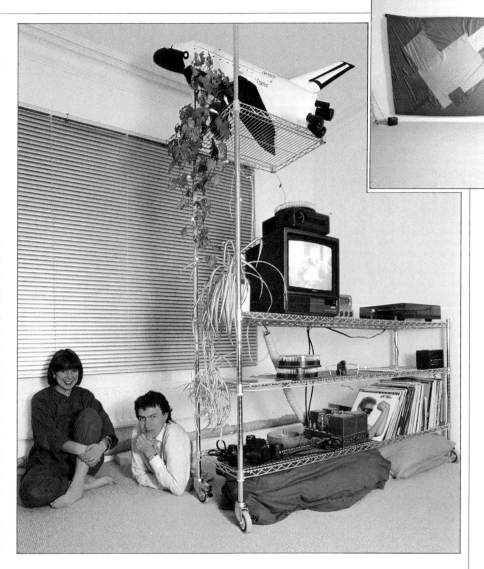

North London apartment. At night, when the sofa is wheeled away, the bed is unhooked from the wall support. Adroit space engineering is essential when one room plays many parts.

Sometimes you will want to make a clear distinction between living and sleeping areas. Either use screens and room dividers that mark off boundaries in the room, or demarcate a sleeping area from a seating area with a simple rug. Beware of using too many different patterns in a small floor area lest the walls seem to close in on you. Concessions to small-scale living should be in the harmonious background colors of walls and floors, unless you are skilled at painting, in

Architects Christopher Williamson and Karen Maloney are in their North London apartment, with their storage trolley system that can be moved away when necessary. Inset above shows the mattress covered in nylon kite material designed to make an abstract painting when hooked up on the wall by day, in the blue, gray and yellow color schemes of the entire apartment.

These pictures show two views of the living room in the early Victorian London house of Daphne and Joss Graham. Their travels to Turkey and India to buy textiles, flat weaves and rugs for their London shops produced some beautiful pieces which are used decoratively with antique English furniture.

A desk and chair in the corner of the living room is pictured above. Cast-iron Punch and Judy figures hold back the shutters that are painted white in a matt eggshell finish to reflect the light. Curtains were never hung because the centerpiece of the room is the eighteenth-century French needlework rug with its autumnal colors that suggested the color scheme, and conflicting patterns in a small room can become too dominant.

Apricot, russet, coral and a hint of green are the harmonizing colors of the living room. The wall color colour was inspired by Portuguese houses that are washed each year earth color. Daphne Graham mixed terracotta, umber and yellow powder paint into a little white emulsion with water and dragged it swiftly across the walls. This fast-drying technique gives a dry look which comes alive at night. The new floorboards were stained with earth colors before the rug was laid to give a grain and make the floor lighter.

which case *trompe l'oeil* (the art of deceiving with three dimensional painting) can create magical vistas. In this way you can create a harbor view from your modest apartment, the balustrades of the terrace from which you view it painted in the foreground. Rather than let color and pattern dominate in one room, choose a tranquil monotone setting that gives the impression of space. Understated backgrounds allow different zones to be highlighted. A white ceiling, white doors and shutters, and a mirrored panel inset behind the sofa, or backing the shelving system, all add to the impression of light and space.

Displaying objects

Unlike the kitchen, where display units are mainly functional, the living room needs space for creative visual displays. Use mantelpieces, window sill, ledges, steps, shelves or any other flat surface for a changing display of objects in your living room. Display items that are sympathetic to your theme, such as brass boxes in an oriental setting, sea shells against stone or carvings placed in front of an open brick chimney piece. John Stefanides, who designed the ballroom at the British Embassy in Washington, favors unaffected, yet elegant interiors. He is particularly fond of baskets in the home, and sets them among shelves so that he can enjoy their irregular shape and texture.

Always exercise self-discipline in the display of objects; learn what to leave out, how to avoid clutter and use accessories to add accent color to the color scheme. In Joss and Daphne Graham's living room, red lacquered bowls sit upon a green silk Japanese cloth to emphasize the soft glow of apricot, coral and russet. Daphne Graham, who has been responsible for coordinating decorating schemes for some of Britain's grandest houses, gives the following advice: Weight your color scheme with a touch of bright solid color. Just a hint is needed, for it is the balance of color that counts.

Shelves

These need not be hefty constructions. More flexible systems and those with a lacquered finish add a soft sheen to the background display. Custom-built shelving uses space most effectively if you vary heights by running book shelves across the tops of doors to create your own library. Vary heights with display shelving that runs around the room, low enough to enable you to look down on the objects displayed on it.

Flexible shelving is easy to dismantle and move with you. Choose a modular system if you intend

An unholstered button-back sofa is casually covered with a quilt (**above**) from Kutch in the Thar desert of North Western India, and scatter cushions are covered with Indian embroideries and Cretan needlecraft. An old chintz chair (**left**) stands beside another chair covered in Chinese yellow with a coral bullion fringe and piping. The tablecloth is an embroidered silk Japanese tea ceremony cloth with a collection of red lacquered bowls from Rajasthan. The red lacquer bowls weight the colour scheme with a hint of stronger colour. The fireplace is screened with a floral cutout found in a stall in the Portobello Road. The mirror is a Regency portrait mirror and the embroidery above it is a Toran from Gujarat in India. Its mango-leaf border motif is a sign of welcome in Indian homes.

If your modern house does not have a fireplace, you can install a free-standing type or decorative stove connected to a chimney-flue system on an exterior wall. You can build these systems yourself. Most older houses have fireplaces although they may have been blocked up. Decorative treatments can turn them into a focal point once again.

Designer Ulf Mortiz made a feature of the burnished steel fireplace in dress designers Puck and Hans' house in Amsterdam

(**right**). Fiery-red satin Art Deco chairs set on either side complete the scheme.

Mint green paint, fresh flowers, ingenious side cupboards and a lectern are all designed to distract attention from the fact that this was a fireplace, yet it is still the focal point of the room (**top left**).

The picture (**above left**) shows another fireplace, blocked up yet used decoratively, with a careful grouping of graphics to anchor the diagonal chimney piece painted a pale yellow. The clay-tiled hearth is

an upraised platform. Buttermilk colors in a dairy-style kitchen complement this old cast-iron range (**above right**) restored to its former good looks by its owner, journalist Maureen Walker. A cast-iron stove is set within a large fireplace surrounded by exposed brickwork (**top right**).

stop damp in a sealed chimney. The soaring cost of fuel contributed as much as aesthetic appeal to the return to fashion of the traditional fireplace. It was in 1976 that the National Consumer Council in Britain recommended that no house be built with only one fuel supply: all new houses should have flues.

If you are living in a modern house without a flue, take comfort from the fact that an external chimney can be built on, using the fire-resistant concrete interlocking units that manufacturers claim take less than six hours to assemble. Such prefabricated chimneys are equally suitable for brick- and timber-frame houses. Quick installation of a fireplace opening follows with a fire chamber that can take a room heater, stove, or even an open fire.

If you do have a boarded-up fireplace which you want to reactivate, prise away the covering to see what lies beneath. Hold a lit taper near the opening: if the flame is not drawn toward the vent, the chimney may be blocked and will need clearing by a professional. If it is not blocked, clear away the loose materials in and above the fireplace opening and check the hearth. It will either be a concrete or masonry hearth, with a back hearth below the fireback (which should not be cracked). Old-fashioned chimneys sent most of the heat up the flue, but if you install a throat restrictor you will increase the amount of heat directed into the room. In most countries there is an Advisory Board which will offer practical advice on this matter, and on relining the flue if necessary. However this is a task for a professional.

The first thing to decide if you are unboarding a fireplace is whether to make a solid fuel system self-supporting and run room heaters as well as domestic hot water, or merely to use the fireplaces as a back-up heating system. Many homes today use a fire to take the load off a more expensive system. Choose the method that fits the size and needs of your family. A fireplace is cheaper than other forms of heating, but you do have to keep a fire burning in summer to heat the water. In a mansion this is no problem, but in a 12-foot-square living room it can be insufferable. To minimize the problem, well-designed modern equipment is finely regulated by air control. You can set the fire on minimum so that it is hardly burning, or you can get a blaze going by turning the underfloor draft, or fan, onto the coals. The latest appliances have incorporated a new system to keep running costs low, burning the cheap household coal and retaining the smoke they produce. This smoke is re-burned before emission, entering into the atmosphere as

Bedrooms can be as convivial as living rooms if you are canny. A decorative bamboo bedstead (**above**) makes this bed more like a daybed, and brightly colored cushions encourage daytime lounging. Note the warm coral walls which are such a fine background for delicate pencil drawings. An attractive bedspread and banks of gaily colored cushions will always transform the most utilitarian bed into a glamorous daytime sofa. Fashion and fabric designer Mani Mann's New Delhi bedroom (**right**) is a room in which one can hold court in an informal yet stylish manner. The low bed is covered with Gujarati embroidered cushions, and the furniture made in the style of the Raj. Raj furniture was produced by local Indian craftsmen for rich patrons. Contemporary nineteenth-century European furniture designs were copied and adapted. On the walls is a fascinating collection of Mughal miniatures and Indian glass paintings.

PUTTING FABRIC ON WALLS

Before you start, make a sketch of your room showing doors, windows and power points in place. Take one wall at a time, work out how many panels of fabric you will need and the measurements of each one (allow about 2in/5cm for a hem at the top and bottom, and a small overlap in the wall angle).

Fabric can be stapled onto the wall, backed with an underlay. Alternatively, you can construct a frame of wooden battens, put padding between them and fasten the fabric to the frame.

Tools You will need a heavy-duty staple gun (hand staplers fit flush into the corners of the room, electric ones do not); scissors; contact adhesive; spray adhesive (from art shops); a sewing machine for fabric seams; needle and thread, including a curved upholstery needle; upholsterer's tacks, and a hammer.

Fabric Cotton or polyester padding in rolls up to 6ft 8in (2m) wide; fabric to cover the wadding (flimsy fabric stretches a great deal so settle for a better quality dress fabric if furnishing weights are too expensive in the quantities required); braid or tape to cover the staples.

Working order Always start in the centre (**A**) and work out, cutting separate pieces of fabric to go above or below doors and

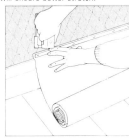

windows (**B**). Finish with the corner sections (**C**).

1. Staple the underlay straight from the roll, just unde the cornic (see above). No seams are needed when butting lengths together — just a small overlap. Cut off flush to the top of the baseboard. Leave the padding ½in (1cm) clear of the edges of the door to allow it to shut properly.
2. When measuring a length of fabric, cut enough to leave a small hem at the top and bottom. If you seam the lengths of fabric together, three at a time, you can cover a large area of wall more quickly.
3. Finish the fabric off in a corner each time, even if you have

enough to reach further as this will ensure better stretch.

4. Lay the roll of fabric on the floor, face down, and start attaching it from the bottom (see above). Turn up ½-1in (1-2cm) of fabric and put a strip of card over it. Staple along the base, through the card, so that when you lift the fabric up the wall you have an inbuilt hem.
5. Put staples, 6in (15cm) apart, along one edge. Work from bottom to top as this makes it easier to get the hang of the fabric right. When you have stapled the bottom edge and one side of the fabric to the underlay, you can smooth out the tension across the width.
6. When three sides are fixed, give the fabric a good pull upwards to smooth out the creases, and staple the top edge of fabric below the cornice.
7. To hide the staples and cover the edge of the fabric, glue

contact tape along the top.
8. For light switches (see below), cut the padding generously away from the fitting, but make the hole

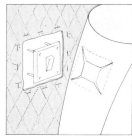

in the material just large enough to slip the fitting through.
9. Staples, or rough edges of fabric, can be covered with decorative braid that either matches or contrasts with the pattern of the fabric. Braid can also be used as a border for fabric panels on doors.
Safety Be very careful when covering walls with fabric as the operation involves working around electrical fittings.

away from the horizontal.

The great restriction to any decorative scheme is space, but fortunately modern houses offer scope for the enthusiastic do-it-yourselfer who can abandon restraint for a more flamboyant style. Fabrics stapled to the walls, swathed over valances, or made up into flounced curtains with a ruffled edge, contribute to the overall effect. Simple supports added to the four corners of a bed can be hung with crackly taffeta curtains, fastened to a central coronet on the ceiling. To this design, add curtains in a watered or marbled silk, generously hung so that they flounce on the floor like the gowns of the period. A striped wallpaper, usually called 'Regency' in contemporary wallpaper collections, is a good base for silver framed photographs

hung from a velvet ribbon, and pictures in gilt frames mounted on a background board of lavender or old rose.

Fabric and color

It is important to consider pattern in the bedroom, although happily the overall coordinated bedroom with everything "mixed 'n' matched" is a fad of the past. Many different patterns can be used in one room, pulled together with plain color, or one pattern can be used single-mindedly.

It used to be a decorating maxim that small rooms could not take large patterns. However, David Mlinaric, Britain's leading interior designer, has exploded that particular myth by taking the Chinoiserie

Bedroom fabrics To give a bedroom a luxurious feel, hang the walls with fabric and use fabric to cover an old screen for extra privacy. It is quite simple to staple fabric onto the walls, as in the bedroom (**left**) with 'Havana', a vibrant design from the Collier Campbell Martex collection of American bedlinen, which coordinates so well with the comforter and pillowslips in 'Nomad' design, from the same collection.

The cabbage-rose coloring of the Romany cotton furnishings from Collier Campbell (**below**) brings country freshness to this urban bedroom. You can copy this simple screen with the minimum of sewing skills. Hem several widths of fabric quite narrowly and thread elastic through top and bottom hems. Then stretch it over an empty frame, which you can make yourself with pieces of 4in × 3in (10cm × 5cm) softwood. The chair, a junk shop find, is painted white and the chest of drawers is enlivened with a hand-painted motif. This attractive look has been achieved very simply, and quite inexpensively, with paints and fabrics.

Scale is of great importance when designing a bedroom or any other room. David Mlinaric, leading British designer, was commissioned by the National Trust to restore and redecorate several grand houses in Britain. In the process, he chose some exquisite old chintz patterns to be reproduced by Tissunique, the French fabric company. To re-scale and in some cases re-color these classic designs took great skill and taste.

The original Oak Bedroom (**right**) at Dunham Massey in Cheshire, was wholly furnished and decorated in 1810 by Henry Grey, 6th Earl of Stamford and his wife Henrietta. From this beautiful room overlooking the ancient deer part at Dunham David Mlinaric copied the charming 'umbrella' pattern of painted cotton, re-scaled it for modern consumption and called it 'Stamford'. He also copied the bold Vitruvian scroll border which coordinates with 'Stamford'. In the original Regency bedroom the window valances which match the bed valances, and the perfectly upholstered 'curricle' chair are particularly fine.

drapes at Castle Coole (a neo-classical mansion in Northern Ireland) as inspiration for his 'Castle Coole' fabric design (see page 174). To promote it outside the world of grand country houses, he used the fabric for festooned blinds in an all-white London apartment. In doing this he illustrated the point that you need never use pattern in a mean way — be generous with a bold print and allow the pattern to take over; this is exactly what is needed in a small room.

Always settle the issue of scale before deciding on your color scheme. There are many different pattern colorways to choose from — ranging from pretty pastels in minty greens and pinks, lavenders, old rose, the limes and grays of Vuillard paintings, to the deep earth colors of old dhurrie rugs and the fresh country colors of porcelain. Designers and decorators talk of "document" colors which means burgundy, bottle green, blue, and mustard on backgrounds colored like spilt tea. Documented colors, taken from printers' archives, always show blue leaves because, in the days of vegetable dyes the yellow, overprinted on blue to give green, always faded. Contemporary colorways faithfully follow that blueprint.

Take another blueprint from the past with a print bedroom. These were once the sewing rooms of eighteenth- and nineteenth-century houses and they adapt well to the scale of modern houses. Black and white engravings of the period, sold by antique dealers as loose leaves from damaged books, are pasted directly on to the walls and framed by cut-out paper swags, garlands, bows and cupids. To complete the print bedroom run a wallpaper border the circumference of

The positive and careful use of color can dictate the entire character of a room, and where is that more essential than in the bedroom — place of dreams, rest, relaxation and creative thinking. The mood has to be sympathetic, and not simply stridently masculine, or prisily feminine. Use pastels by all means, but not to create a sickly sweet confection. White spiced with lemon can be sharp, fresh and bright; blues and grays more demure and elegant. Pink does not need to be irresistably linked to the color of little girl's hair ribbons. Try the subtle shades of salmon, apricot and coral, and match them with pale lavender and mauves. Grey is perhaps the happiest asexual colour in the spectrum. If you are planning a double bedroom, pale grey highlighted with lemon, or steely blue is effective. Or try all white, made extra brilliant with flashes of primary colours.

No man could possibly feel overwhelmed by feminine frills and wiles in this bedroom (**top left**). The steel blue/gray walls are thrown into relief by the pale cord carpet. A superb gilded chair adds a touch of classical restraint to a bedroom that can easily transform itself into a day room. Note the bolsters at the foot of the bed which give it the air of a Regency day-bed.

An all white bedroom (**below left**) is particularly fresh and bright. The almost imperceptible addition of pinky-apricot warms the white to a soft glow. The delightful sloping ceiling is accentuated, cleverly, by its whiteness, as is the pretty fireplace, and the LLoyd Loom chair. A gleaming brass bedstead gives the bedroom the air of a Victorian maid's loft retreat. In any room where natural light is scarce, in a basement, or attic for example, white is a natural choice, as it reflects what light there is far more effectively than a darker shade.

In this bedroom (**below right**) light blue is used as an overall color scheme, with a splash of primary red for dramatic effect. Notice the light-hearted yet practical way in which the dado rail has been used for hanging clothes.

Clean colours have been used in the bedrooms on these pages; clean colours for clean living. Journalist Gilly Love 'hangs for health' American-style from the rafters of her airy loft bedroom (**left**).

Gilly Love works for the British Sunday Express paper. Previously she worked for Habitat where she absorbed many a good idea. Her plans for her loft bedroom were in the main original and characteristic, however. She is a girl who eschews chairs preferring a low profile cushion on the floor, and in the same vein, has chosen a low-level sleeping arrangement, Japanese-style. Caberboard panels (thin chipboard which can be molded at the edges) line the walls and ceiling and have been painted a soft gray, outlined with a deeper gray. The floor is simply standard chipboard, stained a dark gray and sealed.

Bedrooms are also the perfect place to meditate and work. All you need is a little desk/dressing table, like the bamboo table in the bedroom (**above**). Place your desk by the window for maximum light, but beware of distractions if you have an enticing view!

The sunny little bedroom has been painted in the Dulux Yellow Collection. The color Morning Sun has been used on the walls and ceiling, and teamed with Lily White on the cornice and woodwork. For the doorway, the deeper gold of Bamboo matches the bamboo bedstead and table. The bedroom of this 1920s London house (**right**) has been revamped by designer Chester Jones and is loosely based on a 1925 Parisian scheme by Atelier Martine. The walls are stipple glazed off-white, and the fabrics have been specially designed. There are two outstanding points of interest: the Graham Sutherland picture over the bed which dictates the golden colors of the room; and the artificial blossom tree which so effectively breaks up the rather hard line of fitted cupboards. Artificial trees and flowers, made from fabric are in vogue: use them in places where sunlight does not reach.

STYLES OF BEDS

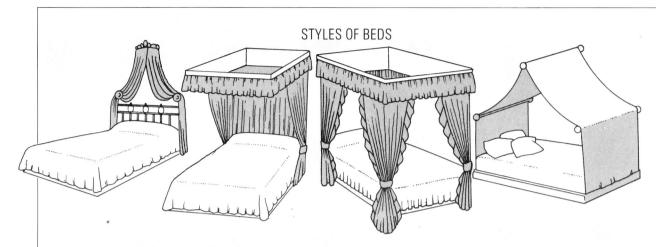

It is far easier to turn the bed into the most important feature of the room rather than attempt to conceal and minimize its bulk. Today you can choose from a wide range of styles, such as antique four-poster beds, beds in oak, brass or painted iron and Japanese style beds.

If you wish to create an elaborate style of bedroom, perhaps with a four-poster bed, and yet cannot afford to buy one, then it is possible to achieve the same effect with fabric alone. Side drapes, coverings and drapes can be hung from poles, tracks or decorative pieces attached to ceilings or walls. The coronet with sheer drapes (**above far left**) is a good example.

Another effective alternative to a four-poster bed is the half canopy or tester (**above center left**). This is supported by two posts at the head of the bed. It is about a third of the size as the fabric-covered ply used on a full four-poster bed. Tied-back drapes hang down either side of the bed and a back drape completes the effect.

Nowadays you can buy excellent reproductions of classic four-poster beds. You can give the bed the full traditional treatment by adding all round drapes (**above center right**).

A canoped effect can also be achieved by bringing a long length of material up from behind the pillows, looping it over a rod suspended from the ceiling, then down to another rod attached at the base of the bed, and finally dropped to the floor (**above far right**).

the room, at dado rail height, to serve as a marker for real framed pictures and gilt mirrors. If this bedroom seems too frivolous, take a leaf from the bookish earnestness and simplicity of a later age. Poet Lionel Johnson lined his study in the early 1900s with brown paper; in the same way you can paste sheets of plain brown wrapping paper directly on to the walls to give groundcover for a collection of sepia photographs in silver frames. In your room, add a mahogany towel 'rack and shoe rack, a wash-stand with a blue and white tiled splashback and a simple iron bedstead. This bedroom, part study, part dressing-room, can house a day bed. British interior designer Mary Fox Linton has one made of bird's eye maple with bolstered sides which can be dressed up in Thai silks from Jim Thompson's silk collection, or dressed down in the Indian calico colours of bleached blue, sand, coral and pistachio.

Soft pastel colours evoke a rural bedroom — a soothing retreat for urban dwellers. The country house style is achieved in a modern house by sanding and sealing floorboards, or painting them white, throwing down a rag rug, and drag washing walls in duck-egg blue or primrose yellow. Hand-crafted fur-

niture, such as a rocker, or a Windsor loop-back chair, or dowry chest for keeping bed linen, will create the right atmosphere. Add the finishing touches with a patchwork quilt, a sampler or tapestry cushions. This is the home for a four poster with white linen sheets and an eiderdown, or a wooden carved bed and Scottish mohair rug. You can add small items to the room to make it welcoming — lavender bunches picked in late summer, drying in bunches on the clothing rails, sprigged cotton laundry and shoe bags hung on hooks, cakes of fragrant soap set inside pinewood drawers to scent them and pot pourri in a porcelain bowl on the mantelshelf.

Actress Shirpa Lane has chosen lace borders as wallcovering to create a nostalgic bedroom in her Paris apartment. Kilometres of lace, found in antique markets, overlap each other in a line along the walls, dappled in colour to suit their antiquity. A filmy gauze, like mosquito netting, frames the bed, and screens the window set in a niche behind. The bed cover is an original 'broderie anglaise' and the pinewood chest of drawers was a junk shop discovery. Often the furniture you have acquired from junk shops will set the style for you. The French call this

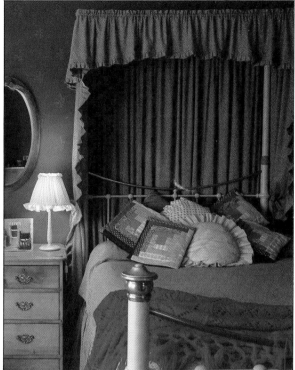

Creative people love designing bedrooms because here you can be as frivolous or as home-spun as you want. Experiment freely with paint finishes and fabric treatments. This gloriously fin-de-siècle bedroom (**left**) is more boudoir than staid sleeping place. Actor Ralph Bates and his wife Virginia run an antique shop in London's Notting Hill area, and theatrical set designers regularly purloin the shop for props. Everywhere lace is used creatively: as borders, fireplace 'fringes', decorative cornices, and valances. Far less voluptuous is this country cottage bedroom (**above**), designed by Norma Bradbury, with its four-poster bed, patchwork cushions and pine chest. Although patchwork is now popular, old pieces can still be bought in sale rooms or junk shops, and stitched onto cushions, thrown over a bed, or pinned to the wall.

respect for tradition 'retro', a term encompassing any aspect from the grandeur of Louis Quinze (a little exaggerated for contemporary living) to the tubular steel furniture of the 1950s. From this era come wire stacking chairs, low-legged teak tables and beds in the Scandinavian style. Abstract geometric patterns on fabric, and a dressing table, swirled in a stiffened skirt of fabric like the dress fashions of the period, complete the decor.

If you prefer not to sit back and rest in a beige bedroom, consider with the curiosity of a voyeur the more unusual bedrooms pictured and mentioned in this chapter. Adapt the ideas you like to fit your own

Children's rooms should be practical but they can be fun and flexible, too. A child likes to feel that his room is his territory, to which he can retreat to read or play. Thus adequate storage, well-positioned play areas, and tough countertops. are a must. Never impose your decorative ideas on children. As soon as they are old enough, discuss with them how they would like the room to look. If red is a favourite colour then it's only fair to forgo your schemes for sprigged flowers and lacy curtains. At least you will inculcate your child with a feeling of responsibility for the surroundings.

There are basically three types of child's room: the baby's room with its cot, changing area and brightly colored mobiles; the under-fives room, with plenty of provision for quite boisterous play; and the older child's room with a sturdy desk for homework, some book shelves, and enough space for TV, stereo, or home computer. The room (**right**) is for a child in the latter category. It belongs to architect Alan Tye and his wife who live in Herefordshire, England. He is half Chinese, she is wholly Swedish — hence the cool and sensible lines of the house. The room that Alan Tye has designed for his son has had to grow with the child's needs: thus the workdesk was once a perfectly servicable changing platform for a baby. The quarry tiled floor is easy to keep clean, and is an excellent surface for running toy cars over. Parents please note that fluffy carpets are a source of great frustration for children attempting to hold the Junior Grand Prix on the bedroom floor.

A blackboard for early morning scribbling (**above left**) has been thoughtfully set into the tongue-and-grooved pine walls and is just the right height for the child. Try to scale children's rooms sensibly, placing mirrors where they can get a good view of themselves, and storing books and toys within arm's reach. A child-sized chair is always popular and most children's shops and department stores stock them.

The problem of sharing a bedroom has been solved by dividing a room (**above right**) into two separate sleeping areas with the help of this brightly colored storage system.

space and impose your own scheme of proportion, scale and color into your bedroom.

Children's bedrooms

You should resist the temptation to use a theme in your child's nursery — he or she may outgrow it faster than your inclination to redecorate. The wise parent will leave the decor relatively simple so that the child can develop an individual character for the room as he or she grows up with it. This does not mean that the bedroom should be unadorned; always be aware of your child's interests. The athletic child with the good fortune to inhabit a high-ceilinged bedroom could enjoy a bed built on scaffolding like a climbing frame with ladders. However, the gentle dreamer who enjoys reading might prefer sprigged wallpaper in pastel colors, an iron bedstead painted white and a small pine dresser or washstand.

Furnishings in the child's room need to be durable, and technological advances in design and printing over the past decade can be used to advantage in this respect. Use modern floor coverings, like foam back vinyl, or sealed cork, rather than a carpet or Indian jute, which scratches young knees and has an uneven surface for playing or building. Small children spend much of their time on the floor and therefore you should consider a surface that is easy to clean and smooth for revving up cars and standing up paper dolls. Some of the French vinyl flooring has games printed on it, but your 11 year old will probably prefer a plainer surface.

Walls should be treated in a matter of fact way as small children have a tendency to unpeel wallpaper. Emulsion paints that sponge off and are long-lasting

If your child is athletic he or she will appreciate sleeping arrangements that can be climbed up to, on to, and swung from. However, bunks or platform beds must be tough to withstand such treatment, as is the tubular steel platform structure (**below**) from the design, manufacturing and retail company, One Off, in London's Covent Garden. One Off make various standard platform beds but will redesign to suit particular needs and color schemes. With growing children versatility is all-important, and what can be a climbing frame which incorporates a comfortable bed for a tear-away six-year-old, can easily be transformed into bed plus study area for a serious-minded teenager.

are the answer and these are good for stick-on glow stars or posters. Magazine design editor Jocasta Innes stenciled holly leaves and berries in scarlet and glossy green along the walls of her daughters' shared bedroom, taking the stencil cut pattern from the American Museum in England. A painted wooden chest to house toys and patchwork quilts in this bedroom added to the folk art freshness.

Hardboard tacked to the walls in giant squares offers good insulation and reinforces the flimsy walls to cut down on noise. You could add a blackboard to the wall, or a tin baking sheet for magnetic fruits and alphabet letters.

Beds and bedding for children

A child's bed needs careful consideration. Bunk beds are a good investment, even for the single child who

will ask friends to stay the night. Always check the bases because manufacturers tend to use an inadequate plywood base to keep the weight down for stacking. This type of base will warp when you turn on the heating for the winter, and the lightweight slats that fit into the wooden frame will snap under the weight of an active bouncer. Equally unsuitable for young backs are those curved cradle bases that you find on carved wooden frame beds. A firm, flat base and a good mattress that can withstand the occasional bed-wetting is ideal. The most suitable bedding for a child is a quilt and fitted sheets — just a shake-up every day and the bed is made. Polyester-filled quilts are best as they are easy to wash and will not cause discomfort to the allergic child, as feather-filled ones can.

Play areas

Children's bedrooms are inevitably playrooms. They can contain such items as work easels and drawing boards which can be folded away when not in use. Folding tubular steel chairs that hang on the wall at a height of 4ft (1.2m) will clear the floor space for complicated games, and you could perhaps erect a long horizontal countertop. At pre-school age it can house drawing books and pens and at a later stage it can become a desk for homework, models that need to be left untouched while they are drying, or electronic games.

Light

Lighting for work areas is crucial. The most useful are the angled clip-on photographers' lights that can be found in most lighting shops, sold in bright colored plastics. They can be moved around the room, clipped on to countertops, and set at the right angle to focus on the work in hand.

Try to ensure that light switches are at a lower level so that children nervous of the dark, or anxious to reach a bathroom at night, can find their way around. Alternatively you can leave a low-voltage light on or place a night-light in the room. You should always have wall sockets with safety shields for lights and gadgets in a child's room — toddlers and young children are inclined to stick fingers and objects into exposed sockets. Track-mounted spotlights above a bulletin board, or around a mirror in a teenage bedroom, provide light where it is most needed. Mirrors can be hung at a height manageable for a child and moved up the wall as he or she grows.

The light source from a window is worth preserving. Blinds usually lose their spring mechanism as

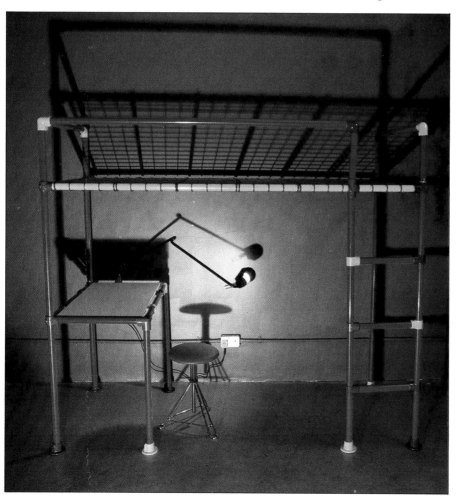

Some houses do not suit the high-tech vocabulary of tubular steel, and in this child's room (**left and below**) a gentler approach has been used. A little attic room can be an ideal hide-out for the very young; children love the atmosphere of these loft rooms with their sloping ceilings and bird's-eye views. The American artist John Canning has quaintly stenciled the floors and painted the little chest of drawers, adding a further element of make-believe. The painted chest (**left**) probably started life as a pretty dull piece of furniture, but it has been given a new lease of life by John Canning. When painting furniture, oil-based paint is best for the background color, and an acrylic paint effective for the decoration.

Stenciling floors is very much like stenciling walls (for technique see page 203). Use graph paper to make a scale model, and adjust patterns accordingly.

your child plays with it, but they are good for daytime resting. Safety sash windows are toddler-proof, but most modern houses with windows that open outward need screening during the early years of your child's life. Vertical bars set across the window look ugly, but are more practical than the horizontal variety that can be used as steps. Later, when your child is older, you can decorate panes of glass with stencil cutouts on transparent paper and they can be colored with felt pens so that they look like stained glass windows.

Space

Modular furniture systems for children, incorporating desks, toy boxes, cupboards and drawers, can provide an interesting island unit to section space in a generously sized bedroom. These units are often expensive to buy, but if you are good at carpentry you could try constructing one yourself.

Hanging space for children's clothes is largely wasted. Jeans, T-shirts, sweaters, socks and underclothing can be stored in a small chest of drawers. Color-matched wire-coated baskets (bought from stores) are excellent for storing items of clothing needed for speedy dressing. Suspend the baskets on low plastic shelves on metal tracks and bracket the shelves firmly to the wall so that they are adjustable. Leave some shelf space clear to display items or collections, whether they are glass animals or

Don't crowd a child's room with too much clutter and extraneous objets d'art, which have no relevance. Leave enough space for an older child's interests to develop: accessible shelves for treasured collections and spacious cupboards for games. The younger child's room needs to be geared to physical activity, so use only simple, durable and washable floor and wall coverings. Chipboard/cork tiles have been painted with wide bold stripes (**far left**) to make excellent railway tracks for these younger children. The walls have been felted for posters and alphabet sheets, and a high gloss door ensures that sticky finger marks can be quickly erased.

An awkward-shaped room (**left**) has been turned into a no-fuss teenage retreat. The slatted wood blind allows maximum light from the tall, narrow window, and a pale colored carpet further lightens what could be a dark room: unwelcoming for quiet study and reading. Under the bed are large box shelves for clothes and games, and an office filing cabinet has been used as the base for a sturdy bedside table which holds a clock and the all-important stereo/tape deck.

SAFETY IN CHILDREN'S ROOMS

Potential dangers to a child alter with each stage of growth and you cannot anticipate every aspect of behaviour that may introduce an unforeseen hazard. The important thing is to deal with obvious and major risk areas before any damage occurs; minor problems can be solved by common sense as and when they emerge.

● Sash windows are generally safe for young children; if the bottom is kept closed it should be too heavy for a child to lift alone. Any window that opens outwards (**left**), whether hinged or pivoted on the frame, is a definite risk, the more so if the child has to climb to reach the catch. Install vertical bars if necessary, sturdy but easy to remove later when the risky age is past.

● Children of all ages use the floor as a play area. Fit smooth, washable flooring and make sure play areas are well-lit. Choose robust furniture in scale with the child and make sure tall units are built-in or bracketed so they cannot be pulled over.

● Keep light fittings out of reach, but place switches where the child can reach them. Any type of fire must be closed off by a child-proof fire-guard. Electrical sockets with safety shutters ensure that a child will not poke fingers into the socket holes while exploring.

● Remove an inside bolt or key from the door of a child's room, as it may cause panic to you both if a child locks the door from inside and then cannot unlock it.

● Toddlers need special care, since they cannot be watched every second. Invest in a stair-gate (**below**), with an adjustable bar so you can fence off stairs at top or bottom. Do not leave a crawling or toddling child unattended in a room with unstable or sharp-edged furniture.

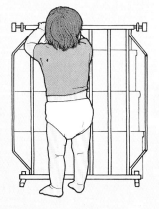

This child's bedroom (**above left**) makes a splendid playroom with its bulletin board for school paintings and brightly colored cupboards for toys and books. Even the track lighting is colorful, with red and yellow lights. Children love bright colors, and do not necessarily appreciate 'tasteful' pastels. Their own exuberant paintings make wonderful wallcoverings: attach a bulletin board the length of one wall, paint it the same color as the other walls, and pin up paintings with brightly colored thumb tacks. Murals have been used in a witty fashion in this child's room (**above**). Large comfy cushions make adequate and flexible seating, and a country pine dresser, enlivened with a Batman poster, houses the TV and toys.

Painting murals on the walls of children's rooms is a good way of pre-empting their own efforts. All children harbor ambitions to scribble on nice clean paintwork. Don't paint your mural upon a porous or flaky wall, however. If possible, apply a base coat of durable, non-absorbent paint. On a base of good low-luster paint use low-luster tinted with gouache, or artists acrylic paints, for the decoration.

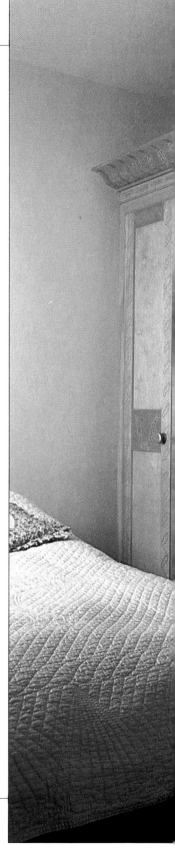

A bank of sleek and faceless fitted cupboards is not everyone's idea of beauty, and the much-maligned free standing wardrobe is making a comeback. Even the ugliest can be redeemed by paint or pretty stenciling. Remember that the free-standing wardrobe, adorned or unadorned, can move when you do. An awkwardly shaped room, such as this one (**right**), might not take a free-standing wardrobe, and so wooden cupboards, a bed alcove and shelving have been sympathetically incorporated into the rafters. The rafters also make a splendid frame for a bedroom swing. There is plenty of storage space under the bed and the white shelf alongside is both a useful bedside table and a support for more pine shelves. The use of red (on the blinds, the alcove and the light) warms up a predominantly pine and white colour scheme.

The English artist Fiona Skrine stencilled this charming wooden wardrobe (**far right**). In its original state, the wardrobe was undoubtedly no beauty, but it was at least sound and servicable. Don't waste your time adorning pieces of furniture which are rickety or wobbly. Pine, deal or teak make good backgrounds for artistic artistic license, and you can always 'antique' white laminate by sanding it down and dabbing on paint with rags.

dried seed pods, fish tanks or models. Plastic waste bins stacked beneath shelves can hold bricks and cars, while fabric storage pockets that hang on the wall house soft toys in pouches.

Storage

Many houses are now built with fitted, floor-to-ceiling cupboards in the bedroom and other parts of the house. Although this is a useful, space-saving design feature, it presents a row of doors, against which no furniture can conveniently be placed. However, if you do have to live with built-in cupboards, you can use a variety of tricks to make them part of the decor. Paper the doors in the same paper as the walls or paste on wallpaper borders that edge the cornice and baseboards around the cupboards. To distract the eye from so much frontage, add window shutters (they don't have to work) and draw them back against the wall on either side of the window. Paint them the same color as the cupboards and panel a section on both the doors and the shutters with a fabric to match the bed linen. You can then frame these panels with moldings.

Louvered doors can be painted so that each slat is a different color, like an open box of crayons. Venetian blinds colored in the same shades will have the effect of widening the room with bands of color. Use an abstract geometric print for the fabric in the room (rather than another stripe) as this will break up the lines, yet preserve the geometry of the whole. Advertisements for fitted cupboards show items stored overhead like airline cargo. Streamline articles for storage behind closed doors, keep as much as possible in the open to add character to the room.

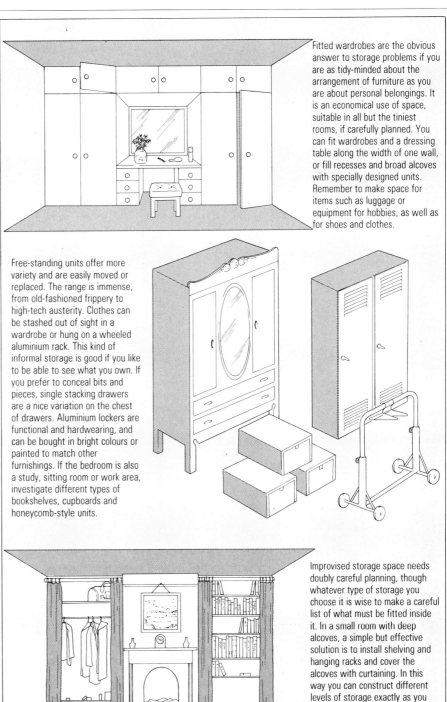

Fitted wardrobes are the obvious answer to storage problems if you are as tidy-minded about the arrangement of furniture as you are about personal belongings. It is an economical use of space, suitable in all but the tiniest rooms, if carefully planned. You can fit wardrobes and a dressing table along the width of one wall, or fill recesses and broad alcoves with specially designed units. Remember to make space for items such as luggage or equipment for hobbies, as well as for shoes and clothes.

Free-standing units offer more variety and are easily moved or replaced. The range is immense, from old-fashioned frippery to high-tech austerity. Clothes can be stashed out of sight in a wardrobe or hung on a wheeled aluminium rack. This kind of informal storage is good if you like to be able to see what you own. If you prefer to conceal bits and pieces, single stacking drawers are a nice variation on the chest of drawers. Aluminium lockers are functional and hardwearing, and can be bought in bright colours or painted to match other furnishings. If the bedroom is also a study, sitting room or work area, investigate different types of bookshelves, cupboards and honeycomb-style units.

Improvised storage space needs doubly careful planning, though whatever type of storage you choose it is wise to make a careful list of what must be fitted inside it. In a small room with deep alcoves, a simple but effective solution is to install shelving and hanging racks and cover the alcoves with curtaining. In this way you can construct different levels of storage exactly as you need them, and use the curtains to bring a touch of extra colour.

If you think of your bed as the centre of operations, then storage should radiate from it. Night time insomniacs should be able to reach out for books or the all-night radio station and the bedside light should be solidly based and not liable to topple over.

The compact sleeping system (**above left**) is from a range of made-to-measure tubular steel designs from One Off in London. Under the bed platform there is plenty of room for hanging clothes, and an alcove space for books and stereo.

Hats, musical instruments and anything else that looks decorative, can be hung on the walls; rackets, umbrellas and walking sticks can be stored in a stand in a corner or hallway.

Another idea for utilizing storage space is to convert a small, spare bedroom into a walk-in dressing room for storing clothes and a dressing table. Alternatively remove the cupboard door in the main bedroom and create an alcove for a dressing table, or place a wardrobe or chest of drawers in the space. Free-standing wardrobes and chests of drawers are still relatively inexpensive because many people do not have room to house them. These could be the only two pieces of furniture in the bedroom, and the chest of drawers can always double up as a bedside table. Trunks and chests can be used as low bedside tables, as well as for storing blankets, linen or ironing. A

cheap pinewood chest of drawers, stripped of varnish, sanded and filled with plastic wood adhesive, could be a decorative item in the bedroom. It will look better painted, but paints need to be rubbed in, wiped off, shaded and scratched to 'age' them. Antique the colour with streaks of burnt umber, mixed into an oil-based paint for a dappled parchment base, then stipple on colour through stencil cuts.

Matching tables on either side of the bed are a nuisance; they usually hold nothing more than a lamp and a bottle of pills. Instead, keep the chest of drawers at arm's length for switching on and off the bedside lamp, or buy a low, wide table. Pillars that support garden statues can also be used to hold a lamp, and these take up far less space. Tables are also useful for housing the television and the lamp, as well as personal items such as photographs and a diary. The

Mobus +, an ingenious sleeping/storage system made by the London firm, Lancelot Furniture, also incorporates a desk (**left**). The unit cleverly combines hanging space, drawers and bed (reached by a ladder), and can be added to, or subtracted from, and moved anywhere in the bedroom, as needs vary. Any child would find such a self-contained 'island' immensely appealing. All units in the Mobus + range are made from high density particle board and covered in magnolia-colored melamine. Blue and pink plastic trimming is optional. Architects Patty and Michael Hopkins have applied their high-tech know-how to solve bedroom storage problems in their London home (**centre**). Behind the bed, screened by venetian blinds, is space for hanging clothes; industrial racks hold bedlinen and shoes. A yellow plastic bedside table swivels about on castors for easy mobility.

simplest way to store a television is on a shelf below a round table top, cut from hardboard. An old quilt covering this and falling to the floor will hide the television when it is not in use. In a modernist home, this would be looked upon as a disguise almost as bizarre as the Victorian practice of covering the legs of a piano. In a modern interior, the television would be on display on open shelving with adjustable brackets to allow the shelves to be moved up and down for items of different sizes.

Heating

For the bedroom, it is worth keeping any heating system that you inherit which is still functioning. Even cumbersome night storage heaters on off-peak timings can have a purpose in a room that is not lived in during the day. Aesthetics have to be tempered by cost, which is why bedrooms are often the coolest rooms in

the house.

Warm air electric heating, pumped from ducts at floor level, is the best-looking system, but it is also the most expensive and it would be rare to find this in the bedroom. Gas is the most common form of heating in the modern house, with radiators that vary from flat convectors to ribbed or modern steel ones. These are flatter and less obtrusive than the electric storage heaters that house clay bricks to hold the heat; however, with gas heating you will need a boiler. Try not to make the error of installing either electric or gas radiators beneath a window. This not only causes condensation on the glass as heat rises, but prevents floor length curtains from hanging properly when drawn.

Apart from a duck-down quilt, and carpeting which makes the bedroom a warmer and more com-

The ideal temperature for a bedroom is warm for the mornings, yet not too stuffy for sleeping. You can afford to keep the bedroom temperature fairly cool, as long as you are cosy under the bed clothes.

If you have a radiator in the room, position it so that it is not too close to the bed, nor abutting wood furniture, or under a window, as this will cause condensation. Peter Farlow has made this simple radiator (**below left**) a work of art by hand-marbling it with paints. If you are not up to hand marbling, you can always smarten up your radiators by painting them the same color as the walls, or even a contrasting color. In this bedroom (**below right**) London architect Piers Gough uses an old-fashioned but functional radiator for a dual purpose. Not only does it warm the room, it also screens the bath from the bed.

fortable place, there is a heating system exclusive to the bedroom. This is the electric blanket — cheap to buy and to install. An electric underblanket that pre-warms the bed an hour or so before it is needed, has to be switched off when you get into bed. Some blankets have an extra warm section at the bottom for cold feet, and the more expensive models have simulated sheepskin covers. Use tapes to keep the blanket flat on the mattress and make sure that you buy the right size so that there is no overhang, as this can be dangerous. The overblanket is designed to tuck in and be left on all night, if desired. Not much heavier than a conventional blanket, it only needs one other light covering.

Insulation

Two unconventional ways of insulating and sound-proofing a bedroom are either to line the walls with padded underfelt, covered with fabric, or with books. Filled bookshelves create a random pattern that is both decorative and warm and a library of paperbacks is a good deal more soundproof than acoustic tiles. The average-sized book requires shelves about 8in (20cm) deep, but since height varies so much, adjustable shelves are a sensible investment. Built-in shelves look best in a clearly defined area that will also house

objects like lamps and ornaments. The wall behind can be painted a bold color or mirror panels can be useful for dressing, as well as reflecting part of the room to give the illusion of space.

There are several different styles of bookshelves to consider: you could have custom-built fitted shelves reaching to the ceiling, above enclosed cupboards, with a ladder to reach them as in a real library. Another idea is to line an end wall around a central window with tracks and adjustable shelving systems, so that the light from the window illuminates the book titles. A more conventional, but attractive, idea is to have white shelves backed with a sprigged motif paper to keep a country bedroom light and bright. The books can be kept in small groups with uprights to divide them. An awkward corner can be made more inviting with two ceiling-high stacks, stocked with books, and a chaise longue or big upholstered arm-chair next to a table and lamp to encourage curling up with a good book.

Use dress fabric for covering the walls as it is the cheapest to buy. It will last for about five years before it looks tatty and needs to be taken down for washing. Back the fabric with cotton or polyester thickening, bought in rolls up to 6ft 8in (2m) wide, and stapled

A four-poster bed creates a sense of timelessness and grace — as well as providing excellent insulation. The bed in the main picture (**left**) has been hung with drapes which are lined with a coordinating fabric. Lined and interlined curtains drastically reduce heat loss. The coordinated fabric has also been used to line the walls, which is another excellent and inexpensive way to insulate your bedroom. Dress fabric is fine for wall-hanging, but to give it more body, and further improve its insulating qualities, line it with polyester or cotton, stapled directly onto the walls. Bookshelves bristling with the latest paperbacks make superb heat and sound insulation at a low cost.

Inside the bed, invest in a good electric blanket, either an underblanket which has to be switched off before you get into bed, or an over-blanket which can be left on with perfect safety all night. Make sure that any kind of blanket is regularly serviced.

Quilts, either feather and down, or all down, have transformed many people's night-time blues. The light feathers (especially the expensive duck feathers) create marvelous insulation without the weight and bother of traditional blankets. If you have an old eiderdown, it is always possible to convert it into a brand new quilt, using the precious down feathers. Comforters, either feather-filled or polyester, are cosy too, and double up as smart bedspreads.

If you are hard pressed for space it is impractical to keep the 'spare bedroom' unoccupied. It is possible to make your spare room earn its keep by giving it another function.

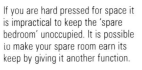

Convert it into a study room, music room, or child's playroom, but site desks, work benches and train sets as far away as possible from the bed so as not to intrude too much on your guests. A bed can double up as a sofa or a storage system and, with care, it will not look too contrived. The Futon Company's sofa becomes a comfortable bed by night with the minimum of fuss (**above and right**). The stylish, low level sofa base comes in single and double sizes and in a natural or black finish.

when the room is unoccupied.

In a very small bedroom, either build in all the furniture so that it resembles a ship's cabin, or try to site hanging space outside the room. In many modern apartments, the corridor outside the bedroom area is lined on either side with cupboards, and this leaves more floor space in adjacent bedrooms. A folding screen in the room will provide a changing space and hide a dress rack for guest's clothes. A small basin can be fitted, with plumbing connections on an outside wall, for guests staying in a one-bathroom household. This is also a satisfactory way of using up corner space. Make the room as friendly as you can with a jug full of flowers, bookends that hold a carefully chosen assortment of books, a towel rack with fluffy towels, a bar of scented soap to make the room fragrant.

If you decide to use the spare room as a study, make it businesslike and organize the desk and seating so that visitors know exactly where to be seated when they enter. Hide-away sofa beds with storage space underneath for extra bedding are very useful, as are beds that fold down from the wall. If budget permits, use sliding panels on industrial tracks to hide a wall of built-in desk space and filing cabinets. Alternatively, buy a range of filing cabinets in primrose yellow, rose pink or green — these are excellent occasional tables and can house all the papers and documents in concertina files.

In a more casual set-up, the spare room could serve a dual purpose as a guest room and sewing room, or provide space for model making or jigsaw puzzles — all these pastimes involve patient construction and bits that have to be left lying about until the final assembly. A large trestle table, covered with a PVC lining makes a good cutting place and work area, with a small separate table and chair for machining and gluing. A full-length mirror can be useful for viewing fashion creations, as well as for guests who want to check their appearance. Site the table near the source of daylight and, as hobbies are often done after nightfall, place a directional lamp on the side to illuminate the subject.

Frequently the spare room is used as a television room and consequently seating is required — anything from floor cushions to sofa beds. If you don't have storage drawers beneath the bed, you will have to house the bedding somewhere else — use a wicker basket with a hinged lid. This can also be used as a table surface for the television, the lamp and any books.

in overlapping pieces directly on to the wall. The average-sized room will take approximately two days to line with material if you have cupboard doors to cover.

Spare rooms

The spare room, as its name suggests, will usually be the smallest of the main rooms in the house. Few people can afford the luxury of an unused room for at least part of the year and it is an unfortunate fact that the guest room tends to become the repository for last year's hobbies and enthusiasms. Plan the spare room as an adjunct to housing friends for a short stay and for giving someone in the family a space to work in

A tiny bedroom (**left**) has been cleverly designed so that there is not an inch of space wasted. There is plenty of room for storage underneath the platform bed, which is screened off from the rest of the room with a nifty wood blind, creating a slightly nautical effect. A fluffy sheepskin rug transforms the bed to a window seat/sofa by day.

The two pictures (**below**) show a apartment which is not ashamed of its dual identity. It manages to look good as a bedroom and elegant as a living room. If you are squeamish about leaving your bed without a disguise in a one-room apartment, then throw over a rug, cushions, or a patchwork bedspread. Alternatively, invest in a really good sofa bed that is as comfortable to sit on as it is to sleep on.

Some beds flap up against a wall and can be concealed by cupboard doors. But perhaps the easiest and cheapest spare bed can be made yourself. Buy two pieces of foam, join them together, and cover with a furnishing fabric. Fold them on top of one another for a sofa, and lie them flat for a double bed.

KITCHENS

Most people have an idea of their dream kitchen. It might be country-style, with a pine dresser, displaying blue and white china; an Aga oven giving comforting warmth to a flag-stoned floor; a large oak table and chairs, papery onions and garden-fresh vegetables on the chopping block — a look that can be achieved in an urban house as well as a farmhouse.

Alternatively, it could be a narrow kitchen, fitted like a ship's galley, with a line-up of white laminated units that conceal ironing boards, slide-away larders and supermarket shelving for utensils. On the stainless-steel draining board lie some frozen shrimp and packages of Chinese stir-fried vegetables ready to go into the microwave oven, the digital clock giving a count-down for the meal in minutes. In short, whatever your taste in food, and the amount of time you spend preparing and cooking it, there are kitchens designed to accommodate your dream.

It was in the 1930s that the concept of the small-scale workable kitchen was introduced, with the utility or galley kitchen being built in small houses and apartments. Later, in the 1960s, when open-plan living came into fashion, the kitchen was opened out to incorporate a diner. Previously the kitchen had been the sole preserve of the household staff, presided over by the cook and the scullery maids, their only connection with the household being the internal telephone and the dumb waiter, the pulley system that transported dishes under silver salvers up to the dining room.

In modern houses the kitchen is the hub of the house. It is the place where friends gather, where homework is done, food is cooked and often eaten straight from the oven. It is no surprise therefore that people devote more time to kitchens than any other room or space in the house.

The prime consideration for any kitchen is function. A good kitchen designer will always ask you how many meals you prepare daily, what kind of food you like eating, the amount of storage space you require and if you intend to use the kitchen as an eating

or sitting area. These considerations determine the choice of fittings and appliances that will furnish the room. Most kitchen manufacturers make fully-fitted kitchens to suit any taste. Units in a colored, laminated finish can house all the equipment you need, but for a grander style these can be trimmed with moldings, Gothic arches or cathedral-style doors. You generally get what you pay for in terms of fittings for spice jars, trays, pots and pans, or a larder. Similarly you can choose solid wood or veneered doors and countertops of marble, wood, or slate. If you cannot afford a fitted kitchen, consider

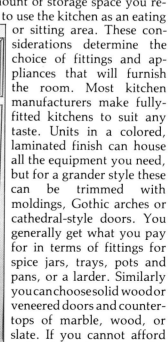

In the last 20 years the kitchen has really come into its own. No longer the 'woman's domain' at the back of the house, the modern kitchen can be a comfortable living room, sophisticated dining area or sleek convenient 'culinary laboratory', in the words of cookery writer and restaurant owner Robert Carrier. The kitchen units (**left**) epitomize the popularity of home-spun kitchen style, which cunningly conives with the most up-to-date modern appliances. The English company Smallbone of Devizes make custom-built kitchen units with a difference. Well-known for hand crafting units in a kiln-dried old pine they now offer a hand painting service. Extra variety is provided by three types of finishes, popular in Victorian times: dragging, stippling and sponging. The units have been exquisitely stenciled.
The Allmilmö kitchen (**right**) however, is pure modern kitchen style with no 'period touches'. Called Fineline Edelweiss it is streamlined for speed with a new modula ceramic system which helped it to win a top German award for good industrial design. The door fronts are covered in continuous pieces of high-quality matt laminate.

Anthropologists will look back upon twentieth-century urban living and proclaim it schizophrenic. Half in love with brilliant kitchen gadgets for fast-freezing, fast-chopping and fast-cooking, we long hungrily for an era when kitchens were cosy, food was fresh not fast, and one dined at a stately pace and not at a gobbling gallop.

This beautiful Connecticut kitchen (**right**), belonging to Bill Norton, owner of the Eighteenth Century Company looks at first glance like a faithful reconstruction of that far away and long ago time. But behind the facade of copper pans and wicker baskets, there beats a twentieth-century heart of stainless steel. The most up-to-date appliances blend surreptitiously with the more traditional components of a 'country kitchen', and they ensure that the cook has time to relax in a room which is as much a living room as a kitchen. The warm glow from polished wood and copper pans draws the whole family into its cosy orbit. Hanging baskets from the rafters provide an endlessly versatile storage system, as functional as any high-tech design. The wood block floor is only slightly more irksome to wipe down than cushioned vinyl, but it is certainly more sympathetic to this expression of solidarity with a bygone age. Everything seems so fresh and airy, so brightly painted that it makes you hungry for home-baked bread, just looking at it.

The German firm Neff have decided to cater for kitchen nostalgia by introducing a luxury electric oven which manages to disguise itself as a Victorian range. This attractive cooker (**left**) is appropriately named the nostalgic oven. Its old-fashioned styling positively encourages you to bake homemade cakes and biscuits. With the superb 'Cirotherm' system you would probably bake at least as well as grandma used to! The brass handle, the clock with Roman numerals and black enamel front disguise the sophistication of the machine: the 'Circotherm' system ensures that hot air is circulated evenly throughout the interior; there is a plug-in variable broiler element and the oven door can be removed for easy cleaning.

open pine shelving for your basic collection of cooking utensils. You can put up shelves for storage jars, stock a dresser with plates, a larder with food and, with a free-standing four-ring oven and a sink you will have the basic essentials for building your dream kitchen.

Choosing equipment

When you plan a kitchen begin with the oven — you can choose from a microwave oven, hot air oven, conventional convection oven with built-in grill and burners, or the ring unit, which today can fit into a worktop only 1¼in (3cm) deep. For urban apartment-dwellers a gas hob allows you to experiment with any cuisine that takes your fancy. It is ideal for puffing out golden *chapatis*, held with tongs over the naked flame, or for blistering the skin of fresh eggplants so that they impart a smoky flavor when crushed into a spicy North Indian vegetarian dish. In the country an Aga can be a constant source of heat for the copper kettle, biscuits warming in the bottom drawer and a stock pot for soups, the top rings large enough to hold great preserving pans for pickling and preserving the farm produce of summer. Thus needs, and cooking styles, change.

Modern technology is not incompatible with a

Aga (**above**) lends its reassuring authority to a country-style kitchen. Agas have been around for almost 60 years, yet their popularity has not waned. Indeed, for people wanting to re-create an old fashioned kitchen atmosphere, the presence of an Aga is an instant stamp of approval. Agas can be gas or oil fired, or fueled by coal, coke, wood (and virtually anything else which is combustible). An Aga comprises several ovens of different sizes and a large ring area. If kept alight 24 hours a day, it successfully uses its stored heat to cook; the ring is always hot enough to boil water in a trice and it keeps the kitchen snug and warm.

SAFETY IN THE KITCHEN

A kitchen contains many potential hazards and some degree of risk is inevitable owing to the nature of necessary kitchen tools and appliances. But attention to detail in planning the fixtures and appliances you will need can greatly reduce the risks.

● The stove is the primary danger. Look for child-proof controls, a guard rail around the rings (**see right**) or rings only at the back of the unit, so that pans cannot be easily knocked over or pulled down.

● Keep a small fire extinguisher to hand, specially equipped to deal with kitchen fires. It only increases the danger to douse burning fat or electrical elements with water.

● Place electrical appliances on a stable surface out of reach of children. Keep wires and plugs well away from the water supply.

● Fit electrical sockets with safety shutters. Don't overload sockets by running several appliances into an adapter unit.

● Install adequate storage space so that countertops do not become cluttered. Keep sharp and pointed kitchen tools separate in specially designed racks or drawer divisions.

● Provide good lighting over the main countertop.

● Fit well-finished shelves and cupboards, with no jutting corners or rough edges, at a convenient level for safe and easy use. Fit efficient catches to cupboard doors.

Neff's Circotherm (**center left**) is a single oven with microwave set into the unit space above. Microwaves are a marvelous invention for fast cooking and, used in conjunction with a well-stocked freezer can save a busy cook hours of preparation and cooking time.

Microwaves can be set into the unit display, as shown in our picture, or they can stand like a medium-sized TV on the countertop. The Neff microwave 6006 has a triple safety door interlock system, special 'stirrers' for turning the food and a meat temperature probe.

The kitchen (**left**) has a split-level oven and hob system with a fume extractor. The advantages of split-level cooking are not necessarily space saving; indeed in a small kitchen a conventional stove is probably your best bet. However cooks like the ease with which they can prepare food around the ring unit. Split-level rings are also versatile: it is possible to have a combination of gas burner and electric plates. You can also have a gas/electric mix or deep fryers and plate warmers set into the ring unit. Some models have covers; others have a special ceramic finish which is so hard you can use it as a chopping board when the heat is off.

country-style kitchen: an agreeably rustic exterior can disguise an up-to-date oven. The German company Neff, for example, produces the Nostalgia range of electric hot-air ovens with a dark enameled front and small oval glass panel, brass towel rack to hold the tea towels and roman numerals on the timer. Range hoods in wood, with recessed shelves on either side for the display of pretty china jugs or plates can fit into awkward corners over built-in ovens (like old ovens built into the chimney piece) and this will add to the illusion of the up-to-date country kitchen.

The most advanced stove is the microwave. These cause the molecules in food to jostle each other and create instant heat, so that it cooks in one-quarter of the conventional time. One minute on defrost thaws out deep-frozen food. Jargon such as 'computing your program for the oven in reality means setting the timer according to the recipe in a special cookbook that accompanies the microwave. Some microwaves have revolving turntables to set the food turning round inside, but the real revolution, universal to every microwave, is in the cooking utensils. Paper dishes go into the microwave oven; so do plastic bags, roasting bags and glass. Anything metal overheats and spoils the food, so all those cast-iron pans are relegated to the ring. Sauces can be made in an instant without stirring over a double boiler. The ingredients tipped raw into a glass measuring jug, will set to perfection in the microwave — just one whisk as it cools down and the sauce is ready. Unfortunately microwaves will not brown food, although they roast, braise and bake. Even with the special browning tray that you buy with the ovens, most recipes for microwaves use paprika to color, as well as flavor, chicken dishes.

Hot-air ovens also cook faster than the more conventional oven, at lower temperatures. An element at the back heats the air inside the oven instantly and a fan circulates the hot air through ducts. The same effect is achieved by baking or roasting in a microwave as spit-turning in medieval kitchens.

Ring units with multicolored tops, or in stainless

steel, may be set into countertops. They can be gas or electric, or a combination of both. Two other gadgets — the barbecue grill and the deep frier — also fit into the countertop and enable the cook to try more adventurous menus than fish and chips. Beignets and batters, Brie in breadcrumbs and jam doughnuts are just some of the recipes contained in the booklets that accompany these appliances.

Planning a kitchen

Ergonomics, the wonderword that came into its own in the 1960s, about the same time as open-plan kitchens, made a great issue of labor-saving planning in the kitchen. The easy formula to remember, without a tape measure, and involving only commonsense, is to place plumbed-in items like sinks and washers against the outside wall if possible, and keep the work area compact. Every kitchen has to be equipped to cover various functions: storing food and utensils, preparing and cooking meals, and sometimes space for dining. The cooking area should be close to the cooking pots, and the refrigerator and work surfaces should be nearby. Kitchen planners who draw up plans of a kitchen for you, should provide an estimate and make suggestions that will fit into your budget. They will install the kitchen units, but they do not necessarily make connections for the essential appliances. Always check whether plumbing and electrical work is included in the estimate as it can be very expensive. You should specify whether a pantry and laundry is to be included in the fitted kitchen area, as well as listing all the things you need — from hideaway ironing boards, fold-out tables, sliding cabinets for saucepans, tall cupboards for ladders and vacuum cleaners, or space for gadgets, such as mixer, coffee-grinder or pasta machine. Different room layouts open up the possibility of planning your own space. Perhaps you already have units fitted, in which case you could consider the addition of a butcher's chopping block, or a marble pastry slab; a central island unit to house a ring unit, or a breakfast table and chairs.

Individuality in the kitchen

If you are remodeling your present kitchen or instal-

A three-sided square of units has been built into a large studio space (**right**), creating a room within a room. The sink, with a narrow drainer, has been positioned opposite the ring unit and oven. In order to save space they stacked one on top of the other. There is plenty of surface space for preparing food and ample storage space in the deep units is created with room dividers.

The cookery writer Prue Leith has a totally original round work-table, part chopping board, part storage cupboard in the middle of her large kitchen (**far right**). This is the center of operations with cupboards, shelves and drawers recessed into the base of the work-table. In the center is a tiered structure of revolving shelves for herbs, oils, knives and wooden cooking utensils.

KITCHEN PLANNING

THE KITCHEN TRIANGLE

When you are planning your kitchen, remember that there are three essential fittings — the sink, the cooker and the refrigerator. Ideally these should form a work triangle with the sink along one wall and fridge and cooker in the two corners opposite. Lack of space and other irregularities sometimes make this arrangement impossible, but try to place these items at an equal distance apart (but not too far apart) so that there is enough room within which to work.

The following schemes show how the work triangle can be organized in different kitchen layouts.

Scheme 1 This plan is for an 'E'-shaped room with the window on the long wall. To make the most of daylight, place a dining table in front of the window and separate it from the kitchen area with a low counter projecting across the room. Behind this counter, line up units to house the sink and cooker. You could emphasize the dining area with a change of flooring — from

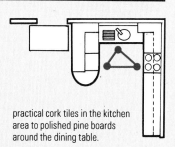

practical cork tiles in the kitchen area to polished pine boards around the dining table.

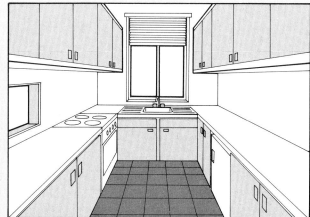

Scheme 2 This is another long, narrow room, with the window at the end of the tunnel in front of which it is wise to place the sink as there is not enough space to push out chairs. Line up units, along both long walls, to house appliances and foodstuffs. On the side with the cooker, put a hatch through into the next room to let in more light and 'unbox' the space.

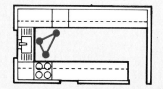

Scheme 3 In a small square room, the 'L' layout is an easy one, using one wall for a line-up of units and part of the next for a round-up of cooking units and storage space for pans. The dining table can off-set the 'L' shape if placed on the opposite side of the room, and the tip of the 'L' can be made into a feature with a barbecue grill, or snack bar.

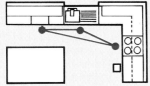

Scheme 4 In another square room, more generously proportioned, consider a central island to house the hob and the sink. Set ceramic tiles over the worktop, or use slate, or a non-porous marble-like material called corian. Add architectural distinction to a featureless room with a handsome cooker hood and display the cook's utensils alongside — a length of copper piping or a rafter will do, bordering the hood at its base. This circular or square hood brought down from the ceiling can have the extract pipe inserted between the ceiling joists and taken to the outside.

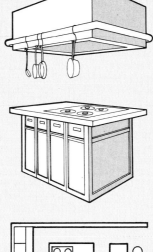

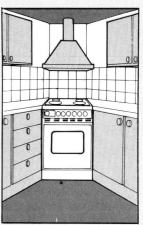

Scheme 5 Make a feature of an awkward corner without losing cupboard space in the angle by placing the cooker into a corner display unit. Overhead cooker hoods, like funnels, will create the impression that it is built into a chimney breast.

The kitchen (**near right**) was specially designed for Robert Carrier's London home by Smallbone of Devizes. The elegant units with their dragged blue finish, coordinated with terracotta interiors, would not look wrong in a living room. This is exactly the effect Robert Carrier wanted to achieve — a kitchen that is at once functional and beautiful. The cupboards can store his extensive 'batterie de cuisine' as well as display his lovely collection of old Spode china. Friends can sit on the comfortable and prettily upholstered window seat nearby and watch their host prepare a gourmet meal. A central peninsula work area incorporates a double sized hob and two separate double sink units. An original butcher's block alongside is the best possible chopping board, leaving the white Corian countertops free for stirring, grating and whisking, as well as for displaying the decorative kitchen items Robert Carrier treasures for their looks as well as for their practicality. The floor has been painted a deep Delft blue (to match the cupboards), and the border is trompe l'oeil. The kitchen (**far right, top**) has a more electric feel with its traditional free-standing stove and attractive mélange of old and new styles and ideas.
The kitchen (**far right, bottom**) however is deeply rooted in the 1950s style. The units are original, as are the kitchen table and chairs. Vibrant oranges and blues give it a brash yet confident feel.

ling a new one, you may have to remove old appliances, tiled surfaces, even walls. If you plan to update your kitchen on a piecemeal basis, the best course of action is to plan it thoroughly around the colors already present and add a few free-standing items, such as a dresser.

A quaint style can be introduced to a dull kitchen by painting simple and cheap units a duck-egg blue. Dab a matt yellow onto the walls, varnish them with matt varnish to bring up a patina and hang up some still-life prints. Bentwood chairs stained a deeper blue, with perhaps a patchwork cushion tied to the cane seat and a maple table will give the room a distinctive air. Robert Carrier's kitchen is personalized with light blue painted units, dragged with coats of a deeper blue to match his blue and white Spode porcelain collection. The walls and the backs of the open shelves are painted terracotta, which suits the earthy shade of the cast-iron ware he uses for cooking. The floor is painted a deep Delft blue to match the cupboards.

Many manufacturers nowadays offer services that add individuality to the fitted kitchen. The units are usually delivered to your home with just a base coat; once installed, they may be stenciled or hand-painted with Victorian finishes such as stippling or dragging. The introduction of an unexpected texture or pattern will break up a conventional line of units. Alternate units of varying heights, an idea borrowed from designer Max Clendenning, can look more interesting than standard ones. In a custom-built kitchen, he staggered the heights of units from floor to ceiling-height to countertop-height, painting the ceiling a glossy red, the units matt gray. If you get a brochure from your kitchen unit manufacturer you can see how to introduce different units or door fronts in bold colors to break the existing line-up.

Described as the maverick of kitchen design, British kitchen planner Johnny Grey says: 'Fitted kitchens have so little pedigree that clichés are foisted upon products to provide them with an image. Timeless wonder, space-age fantasy, streamlined efficiency are just some of them.' His answer is to design individual items of furniture around each of the main kitchen functions: a sink unit, a storage dresser, a chopping block, open shelves, a suspended ceiling around which cooking utensils are hung, a central counter, even a special stove, all drawn together by some original architectural feature, such as a chimney piece or cornice.

Other enlightened kitchen manufacturers offer kitchen furniture that avoids the row of units. Pieces

include court cupboards, endgrain chopping blocks, white ceramic sink cabinets in the Edwardian tradition, plate racks, wall-mounted storage units for china, or open shelves with ornate brackets to house tea caddies or spice jars.

Nick Ashley, a designer for the successful fabric house of Laura Ashley and son of the same, keeps all his kitchenware — and a great deal besides — on long shelves firmly bracketed to the wall of his London kitchen. Such a system demands a good-looking array of objects, but most cooks are keen to keep the equipment they use out in the open. A softer approach to open shelving is to paint the walls plum red, and just within the perimeter of the shelves, pin a paper-cut along each shelf-border to emphasize a country-kitchen store of preserves in glass jars and homemade fruit butters and jellies.

The last word on kitchen preferences comes from cookery writer, Jane Grigson, whose choice of fully fitted units is from the Wrighton range — a Delft blue-gray laminate with wooden door, painted white, that conceals a spectacular larder. Jane Grigson would add a conservatory next door to this kitchen, as well as tracked doors that slide across the sink area .

Sinks and washing machines

Kitchen planners claim that, ideally, 3ft (1m) should be left at the side of the sink for piling up dirty pots and pans, and 2½ft (76cm) for draining the clean crockery. The oven and ring unit should be no further than 6ft (1.8m) from the sink. However the ideal juxtaposition is hard to find, especially when one considers the importance of siting the washing machine and the sink on an outer wall for easy plumbing. Often this is impossible.

Those smart, pastel-colored, oval sinks become irrelevant when you find you cannot fit a turkey roasting tray inside one. A double sink is a good idea, if there is room. Once the preparation is over, one sink can be used for rinsing, one for washing up. Between times, you can cover one sink with a wooden chopping board to stop things toppling in, and to provide extra work space if you need it. A handsome version of the double sink is the old-fashioned butler's sink, until recently, a prize find on demolition sites. Today, they are manufactured along with reproductions of claw-footed baths covered in the same white enamel. As with the baths, no pretence is made of hiding the plumbing pipes, which become an intrinsic part of the design, but with all the advantages of contemporary plumbing.

Underneath the sink a unit can house the bin and

Cookery writer Jane Grigson chooses Wrighton's Delft range (**above**) for a fresh bright kitchen decor. The white painted wood frames and pale gray laminate cupboard panels may look heavenly but they conceal a fiendishly ingenious system of pull-out racks and down-to-earth shelving ideas. A special pull-out larder activates at the touch of a fingertip and, as seen in the picture, it is conveniently placed for both the working and dining parts of the kitchen. Extra paneling has been used to make a free-hanging chimney hood to keep the kitchen smelling as fresh and clean as it looks. A central 'island' unit combines a ring unit and preparation area, and is placed near the dining table for conviviality.

An old fashioned earthenware sink (**above left**) has been preserved not just for nostalgic reasons, but because its size makes it supremely functional.

The rectangular double sink unit (**above right**) incorporates a waste disposal system between the two sinks. Expert dishwashers love double sinks, because they can soak dirty dishes in soapy water in one, and rinse them off in the other. Put a chopping board over one of the sinks and you have the most practical system for washing and peeling vegetables.

The white single sink/drainer (**left**) has a large 14 × 15in (35.5 × 39cm) bowl with handy crockery basket (used here for washing and draining vegetables). Other accessories available include a teak chopping board and Luran draining board. Between sink and drainer is a handily positioned waste disposal unit.

Enthusiastic cooks like nothing more than to display treasured gadgets, pots and pans. An industrial shelving system (**above**) makes a splendid open cupboard.

A well-stocked and ventilated larder with produce clearly visible is sadly a thing of the past. Refrigerators have usurped the place of the larder in the modern kitchen, but the very low temperatures of refrigerators can ruin things like creamy bries, eggs, and crisp lettuces. In response to a real need, the German firm of Bulthaup has developed this food cupboard (**above right**), with versatile shelving on a grid system on the doors, and masses of interior space for vegetables and wine.

the indispensable plastic bucket. Somewhere near the sink (if you do not have a separate laundry) you should plumb in the washing machine and dryer, either combined in one machine, standing side by side, or one on top of the other. Buy the best machine you can afford; during the full cycle of rinsing and spinning, machines develop a whine and can walk across an uneven floor — only precision engineering will ensure the calm, smooth performance you expect from such a bulky machine.

Storage

There are many items to be stored in a kitchen, from appliances to chinaware, glassware, cutlery and cooking utensils, so that plenty of storage space is essential. Decorative pieces, such as china cups and plates, look good on open shelving, either on a dresser or in wall cupboards with glass fronts, or leaded diamond pan lights. A huge dresser piled with an assortment of plates, including porcelain and junk shop buys, is the idiosyncratic storage piece used by designer Susan Collier of the Collier Campbell fabric-design team. A cook's equipment should always be close at hand. Keep the mixer, coffee grinder and sandwich snack-grill on the countertop. If you have a pasta machine, clamp it onto a work surface near the pastry slab. The icecream maker can hibernate in a cupboard during the winter and spend the summer whirring away in the fridge, but few items are so agreeably seasonal.

It is the collection of small items that clutters up a kitchen. Josceline Dimbleby, author of the Sainsbury's supermarket cookbook series, finds Habitat's plastic-coated wire grid, hung alongside the splashplates above the countertops, very useful. On

Diana Phipps has solved the 'should it all be on view or not' kitchen storage dilema in the wittiest fashion. In her magnificent old kitchen (**left**) she has painted still-life portraits on her cupboards of tempting delicacies, and elegant kitchen paraphenalia. Copper pans, bowls of fruit, bunches of herbs and a collection of books hide, perhaps, more mundane articles such as the lemon squeezer or food processor. If you are not artistically gifted enough to execute such elaborate trompe l'oeil effects, simple stenciling on plain wood or laminate units is surprisingly easy to do. Or just paint your units an outrageously un-kitcheny color such as pale pink. dark lavender or black. Pretty posters of fruit and flowers are often unit sized. Stick them onto the front of your cupboards, and protect them with a polyurethane varnish. Remember to use a water-resistant adhesive.

this can be hooked ladles, and baskets to house spoons, whisks, bean peelers, and garlic presses. A knife rack for stainless steel and carbonated steel knives is also useful in the food preparation area or you will end up using the same knife for every task.

Neat ways of hiding all those tiresome mops, dusters and vacuum cleaners are provided for in kitchen units. These range from ceiling-height broom cupboards to a baseboard pull-out panel for the shoe-cleaning kit. An excellent solution to storage in the small modern kitchen is the practical wall-grid system — a series of criss-cross wire frames attached to the wall with baskets and shelves attached to them. The various containers are fixed to the grid with clip screws and plugs, fitted vertically or horizontally, to house a variety of items including bottles, tins, mugs and jars, tools and utensils, even cookery books.

These unusual, yet entirely practical systems come in a range of colors to tie in with your kitchen scheme.

The refrigerator is the conventional place for storing food. It can be concealed behind a unit front that matches the rest of the kitchen, decorated with enameled magnets, or painted decoratively using enameled paints. Decorator Diana Phipps has painted an attractive still-life of copper utensils, fruit and wine on the glass panel of her oven and the white refrigerator door in her Cotswold country kitchen.

Changing-room lockers, generally sold to schools and games clubs, offer an unusual yet practical pantry. Track doors fit into each other in sections, which saves corridor space, and the clothing rack provides hanging space for pots and pans, colanders and sieves. Bolt-on metal shelving, covered in red PVC, which can be sponged down, can hold the foodstuffs and china. Each locker has its own combination of straight shelves and rods, arranged so that every inch of space is used without stacking.

More conventional, ventilated larder units, marketed as mini-markets in kitchen books, have crates for cold drinks at the base, a cold shelf for dairy produce, wire baskets to house foodstuffs, and carousel shelving that hangs from the central hinge of the folding doors.

Gadgets of limited usefulness, such as electric can-openers, which hint at processed foods containing artificial flavorings and unhealthy preservatives, have given way in many kitchens to mushrooms in a plastic bucket, bean sprouts in muslin, or parsley in a pot — examples of the modern trend toward more fresh foods. Pots of peppery basil, fragrant thyme and sage are set on window sills, cress grows on a washcloth, runner beans trail their scarlet flowers around the kitchen window in late summer and city-dwellers see the value of a constant supply of red salsify and bright green corn salad grown in window boxes in rotation.

Anton Mosiman, head chef at the Dorchester Hotel, London, keeps a trout tank in his kitchen at home, stocked ready for cooking and eating. He also likes to make his own fresh pasta. John Lewis of Hungerford, who built Anton Mosiman's kitchen, made a pasta table on top of a trellis store of wine bottles so it acts as his wine cellar as well. The pasta machine is clamped next to the corian (fake marble) worktop and churns out strips of tagliatelle and fettucine or flat boards of lasagne.

Countertops and wallcoverings

Cupboard ranges can be pulled together with a solid wooden countertop, custom-built to fit your kitchen. Wood makes an excellent chopping surface and ages well. Ceramic tiles are also popular for countertops, although they must be grouted with a heavy-duty, non-porous tile grout — you could use a bold color. You could tile your own tops, but ensure that you have a plumb line with a spirit level before you begin. Then all that needs to be done is to rub down the surface with glass paper, stick down the tiles with adhesive, and grout in between. Sealed cork flooring tiles can sometimes be used to cover countertops but they are not heat or water resistant.

Pastry-making or rolling requires a cool surface. A marble board with a cork base will do, though it is seldom big enough for rolling out, so a separate section for pastry- and pasta-making is essential for the enthusiastic cook. Corian is a new material that looks

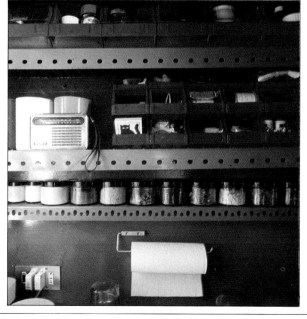

There is nothing more aggravating than hunting out that bottle of special vinegar, that jar of dried beans, or the one egg cup in the house, when you are in mid-cooking bustle. Worse still is having to search in dark cramped cupboards — with your head wedged inside and your arms flailing about knocking over sticky sauce bottles, you may well feel that your storage system is ready for a rethink. What could be simpler than Bulthaup's white shelving (**top far left**) that can be shifted and adjusted on the paneled wall, as desired. Place on the shelves the things you use regularly and therefore wash every day. Occasional crockery will only get dusty and grease-streaked and have to be washed off before use. Metal industrial shelving (**bottom far left**) makes open shelving a really practical consideration. Team it with plastic containers, usually used for storing screws and nails in the workroom.

A lovely old pine dresser (**bottom center left**) provides a mellow and sympathetic background to a collection of old china. The deep cupboards at the base can be used for tins, bottles, freshly laundered table linen, or even children's toys. Kitchen drawers are rarely the right size. Either they are so big that the tiny cookie cutter is irredeemably lost, or they are so meanly dimensioned that big items have to be wedged in. Belthaup's Vario cupboard (**near left and below**) should solve most people's problems. The cupboard has drawers and shelves in a variety of shapes and sizes. Some drawers are capacious enough for packages of tea or cookies, others small enough for candles, scissors or napkin rings. Made of either beech or oak, the Vario cupboard looks as much at home in the living room as it does in the kitchen.

There was a time when a table cloth was de rigeur in every kitchen. Unfortunately we have all become too lazy and too fond of modern wash-down surfaces to bother with such niceties. It is, therefore, refreshing to see a well-laid kitchen table in a small studio (**right**). The fabric used for tablecloth, napkins and blinds is Castle Coole, one of a selection of fabrics in the National Trust Collection, chosen by David Mlinaric and sold through Tissunique Ltd., and Prelle et Cie of Lyons. The elaborate chinoiserie design is an exact replica of glazed chintz used for the window curtains in the Bow Room at Castle Coole, Northern Ireland. Too grand for a humble little kitchen? Strangely, rescaled and in a crisp blue and white color way, Castle Coole is charming. Note, too, the smart black and white tiles for walls and splashplates, and the original Victorian tiled floor.

like marble but is stain-proof, reasonably heat-resistant and non-porous. Consider topping a single unit or free-standing island unit with a corian surface.

Wallcoverings and paint surfaces should be easy to clean too. Use a silk emulsion, given greater character by sponging stronger color over the top, and rubbing on the paint with a piece of material so the base coat shows through. Alternatively try brightening up wooden units with paint and stencils. Oil-based paints are the most durable, but emulsion is easier to use. For stencils use acrylic paint thinned with water, or a silk emulsion. Matt lacquer will protect them. In a laboratorylike kitchen with stainless steel drainers, caterers' utensils and microwaves, paint the walls a high gloss white and then varnish. This sort of kitchen will suit Letraset lettering on the unit doors, spelling out the contents — 'Tea', 'Pasta' or 'Bread'. Vinyl-like brick does not look good over a large surface, but it does add a country look, if used as a backdrop to a collection of cooking utensils on wooden shelves. Laminated cupboard fronts can be resprayed with car paint if you inherit a second-hand kitchen, and window woodwork painted a bold color will brighten up the room, especially with café curtains in a fresh gingham on a brass rod.

Floors

As kitchen floors are subject to scuffing and tarnishing, they need to be durable and easy to clean. In addition to this they should be waterproof, stain-resistant and durable — an exacting requirement but one which is easily met. Nowadays there is a whole range of practical floor covering available from the traditional flagstone floor to the high-tech style of industrial flooring. The cheapest floor covering is vinyl, bought by the square yard. Available in sheet and tile form, vinyl suits a kitchen with awkward shapes as it is easy to lay and to cut to the right measurement. A smart way to evoke eighteenth-century houses, using contemporary technology, is the bold, diamond pattern on vinyl sheeting. Black diamonds cornering white octagonals, or a checked brown and yellow tessellate pattern reproduce exactly the marble flooring in the halls of grand houses, which was considered too smart for the kitchen.

The most expensive flooring is ceramic tiles. If you live in a small house or apartment it makes sense to buy vinyl, but if you are staying put, ceramic tiles are stylish and will give an age-old permanence to the place. Use them also for the walls behind the counter-tops and sink splashplates. The tiles come in a wide

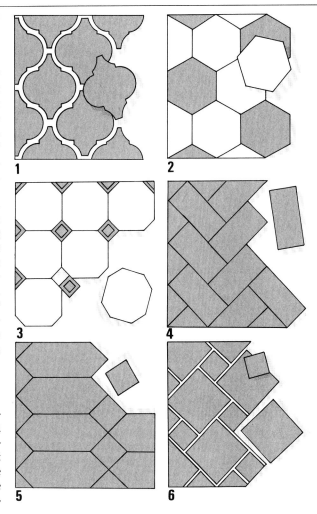

1 **2**

3 **4**

5 **6**

Styles of floor tiling
Floor tiles are available in a wide variety of materials — both natural and man-made, sizes, shapes, colours and patterns. Choose tiles that will suit the style of your room. Warm-toned terracotta and quarry tiles will look good in a rustic kitchen and come in more unusual Provençal (**top left**) and hexagonal (**top right**) shapes. Italian ceramic tiles, which come in many different sizes and colors, can be pieced together to make a patterned floor (**middle left**). A herringbone pattern is suitable for wood block flooring or brick pavers — both these materials are useful for linking the kitchen to an outdoor area. Create interesting effects by using different shapes together for a more intricate pattern, such as narrow hexagons and squares (**bottom left**) or different sizes, small and large squares (**bottom right**). Even plain tiles can be used more imaginatively — use grouting in a contrasting color to liven up conventionally laid plain ceramic tiles, for example, or lay square tiles diagonally to create an illusion of more space in a small room. Remember that the effects created by all these different textures, designs and patterns can be faked by using good-looking vinyl flooring in sheets or tiles.

range of colors and designs, from the witty Italian ones that you piece together to make patterns, to plain earthenware tiles in red or brown clay, fired at a lower temperature.

Expensive brick flooring, whether biscuit-fired or the more common red brick, looks marvelous too, especially laid in a herringbone pattern. Smoky gray slate, the color of Scottish crofter kitchens, is also a good base. You can pick out the paint color on the walls, the perfect background for a collection of blue and white china. Cork, in warm colors, and warm underfoot, has great resilience and, as it is flecked does not show the dirt. The cheaper cork tiles are unsealed and need coats of polyurethane to make them kitchen-proof, but you can use them on the wall to create an instant bulletin board.

The three kitchens on these pages represent three approaches to the modern kitchen. For designers enamored of high-tech or minimalist modernity, the kitchen is the best place to try out schemes. All the most up to date, technologically tried and tested materials are perfect for a room which suffers from more than its fair share of thrills and spills. Plastic, laminates, glass, chrome and metal are all ideal for the use and abuse suffered by the average family kitchen. Vinyl flooring can be wiped down in seconds, melamine shelving, likewise. Toughened shatter-proof glass is a good front for easy-visability cupboards; PVC coated fabric the best and brightest tablecloth when entertaining the under fives.

The bright modern kitchen (**above**) belongs to the fashion designers Puck and Hans. The American architect Fielding Bowman has used wood laminate (**near right**) for custom built 'St. Charles' units which are easy to keep spotlessly clean, yet have the sympathetic appeal of good old wood. The center work-table is on castors to provide a movable feast.

The kitchen (**far right**) is in architect Kroen Van Velsen's own house. It is right at the top of the house and is very light. The whole room has been gutted to reveal metal struts on which versatile shelving can be moved where needed. An Expresso machine provides both instant refreshment, and an object of elegant, even sculptural, interest.

The simplest dining arrangements can be made in a space saving kitchen, using ingenuity and the latest in pull out/flap back/fold away units. Wrighton's Tana design incorporates a useful little pull-out table (**above**): big enough for two to breakfast at; and when no one is eating, useful as an extra countertop. Tana units and table are trimmed in oak framing and the laminate cupboard fronts come in beige or blue/gray.

Fabric designer Tricia Guild's kitchen/diner (**right**) is large enough for eight or more people to comfortably dine. This is a room for cooking, entertaining and working, and therefore there are two tables. Notice the comfortable bench scattered with brightly coloured cushions. At the far end of the room is the table reserved for more serious eating, and should any extraneous clutter hamper the laying of the table, it can all be bunged into the basket suspended over the table.

a cluster of citrus fruits, spring tulips in glass jugs, or little peat pots filled with crocuses. Behind the table, hang vegetable panniers on the wall for extra storage, or paint the edges of open shelves with the border pattern of your chinaware. Give the dining area its own flavor, with a natural arrangement of things, such as strings of herbs, onions, dried flowers hung from their stems, plaits of garlic, even sausages and hams strung up as they are in Italian delicatessens. Wooden butter molds, biscuit cutters or cake tins in your initials can all give character to the walls in your kitchen.

A round table breaks up the framework of units in a kitchen. Emphasize it by changing the floor color or pattern to encompass the ring of chairs. If tiles are laid across the kitchen area, lay them the opposite way under the table. On a tiled ceramic floor, change the color or add a border pattern to break the continuity. Alternatively, you could stencil a pattern on a wooden floor.

A certain intimacy can be added to a dining area by pulling around a screen — perhaps a paneled screen found in a junk shop or made from a length of Liberty 'Near East' chintzes with giant peonies and dragons, tacked into a fold-up wooden frame. The glossy blacks and lacquer reds, with a touch of gray and white, will demand some appropriate table dressing to

accompany them. Perhaps a scarlet PVC table cover, set about with little porcelain tempura bowls and chopsticks, the centerpiece a bowl of cherries in a flat basket.

The dining table makes a statement about your approach to entertaining and style. Remember that no amount of kitchen technology in the planning of appliances and work space can compose your kitchen as well as your own judgement and skill. Remind yourself of some of the impromptu meals that have tasted so delicious without too much planning — kebabs grilled on skewers set between two stones on a picnic, or a red mullet flamed over a dry branch of fen-

nel — and make your kitchen reflect the way you like to live.

Utility Areas

It is a great asset to have additional space in a house or apartment for performing such routine tasks as washing and ironing clothes. A laundry or utility room requires space for a sink or washing machine (both of which need to be plumbed into water outlets) and other equipment, perhaps a dryer, ironing board and baskets of washing. You will also need well-positioned sockets for other appliances.

A sealed-off passageway, if it is wide enough, can

Joss and Daphne Graham's relaxed kitchen/diner (**above**) has been decorated quite simply with white walls, Indian fabrics, a well-chosen painting and pretty baskets fastened to the wall. An old pine dresser holds a much loved china collection, and a dhurrie rug lies quite happily upon the terracotta colored vinyl flooring. This is a kitchen for relaxing in, for unpressurised entertaining, and happy doodling with recipes.

be transformed into the laundry area, using the space beneath the stairs as the ironing section, and plumbing machines to the outside wall. In older houses the scullery converts into a utility room, providing a sink for soaking. Add a counter for sorting clothes and a wall cupboard for detergents, bleaches, bowls and pegs.

Most people fit the laundry equipment into the kitchen area and manufacturers have been quick to see the potential of making appliances on the same scale as the fittings. These are specially designed and colored to match the regular kitchen units and they take advantage of the latest technology for programs and memory recall, without resorting to a laboratory-like decor. If your washing machine does not match the line-up of units in the kitchen, remember that white goods, such as the refrigerator and washer, need not be left white. Use a spray car paint to respray them, perhaps in a dazzling metallic finish or in bold stripes with lines of masking tape to keep the edges straight. Alternatively, you could spray on a stenciled motif and put up a splashplate of plain white tiles, grouted with a color, that matches the background stencil pattern.

Appliances

The needs of your household, as much as the size of your kitchen or utility room, will determine what equipment you buy. A single person in a small apartment will find a cylindrical drum spinner that can be housed in a cupboard space beneath the sink the most suitable machine, whereas a family with active sports enthusiasts will need a washing machine with soaking programs, as well as a separate clothes dryer. The size and layout of the kitchen will also determine whether you have a top-loading machine, a front-loading one that will fit under the countertop, or a washer with a dryer stacked on top. Machine programs vary enormously: they include mixed fabric cool wash cycles with lower spin speed for delicates, hot water soak programs for whites, and economy buttons that switch on to off-peak electricity and reduce the washing time and temperature. Most machines take a wash load of up to 10lb (5kg).

Tumble dryers are either direct vent or condenser dryers. They get rid of dampness by blowing warm air through clothes in the drum. As direct vent machines need to be plumbed into the outer wall, this will determine the site for the dryer; condenser dryers are for use when direct venting is unsuitable. The most sophisticated version is the electronic sensor which

Utility rooms are considered by many to be as vital as a second bathroom. They certainly remove the less attractive appliances such as washing machine, dishwasher or freezer from the kitchen and leave more leeway to create a pleasing kitchen design.
Photographer Michael Dunne has a laundry room in his London home (**above**). Appliances are tucked away under a useful countertop, above which there is plenty of room for clothes to hang dry. Folding louvered doors pull out to cut the whole area off from the rest of the kitchen.
Space in a hallway has been cleverly used to make this laundry area (**right**). A narrow cupboard has also been built in, for storing such unsightly objects as detergent and fabric conditioner.

A small laundry room and a downstairs lavatory lead off from this kitchen/diner (**left**). Many people dislike mixing clothes laundering with cooking and eating for more than aesthetic reasons. They rightly feel that the grease in the air of most kitchens will adher to freshly washed clothes. Besides, it is nice to be able to wash, dry, mend and iron a batch of clothes in the same room. In that case, turn your utility room into a laundry, and send the dishwasher and freezer back into the kitchen. If you don't have a utility room, then it is always possible to partition off a section of the kitchen with folding doors, or even venetian blinds. In the picture (**left**), a sense of unity prevails by tiling throughout with the same color ceramic tiles.

dries clothes to the exact point required, depending on the fabric and the load. Other appliances that can be kept in the utility room are the deep freeze and the dishwasher. Once considered a luxury, the dishwasher has justified itself as an essential cost-cutter in the home, taking less hot water to wash the plates and glasses stacked inside it than the constant running of hot water to rinse a few items. Dishwashers also relieve the kitchen of clutter as you can stack dirty utensils straight into the unit. Choose a good-sized model that takes dishes for three meals a day.

Flooring
Laundry and utility room floors are subject to much rough treatment, so they must be both durable and resilient. The cheapest flooring is probably the vinyl you lay yourself in a color or pattern which links up with the kitchen floor. Buy the best quality you can afford as you do not want vinyl that tears or splits. Cushion backing will help to deaden the noise of machinery and acoustic tiles on the back of the door will help cut out the whirr of the dishwasher after a dinner party.

Keep bowls and buckets, as well as a simple pull-out clothesline for drying off damp clothes, in the space above the washing machine. Some of the new kitchen unit ranges have pull-down ironing boards with a support strut beneath which you can use to divide space between the laundry area and the cooking area in a combined kitchen/laundry. Clean clothes and cooking smells do not go well together so try to keep these areas as separate as possible.

BATHROOMS

Only three major items — basin, bath and lavatory — need to be considered when planning the basic bathroom. Yet it is the most awkward room to decorate imaginatively. The bathroom interior needs careful consideration: remember that once plumbed, your fittings become fixtures.

Manufacturers claim that soft, light colors create a feeling of spaciousness, whereas dark, rich colors are warmer. Before ordering everything in peach or avocado green, visit builders' stores to look at basins, baths and lavatories in their showrooms. You will be astonished at how much solid color fittings contribute to a room. That small sample shade in the bathroom catalog is much more powerful in three bold ceramic shapes and the impact on the bathroom — often the smallest room in the house — can be profound. Take along a tape measure so that you can see how dealers manage to display fittings in small spaces. Their shop floor has to carry a lot of stock and it is a useful exercise in ergonomics to see how they combine all these features in restricted areas.

According to Robert Sallick, president of 'Waterworks', a company in Connecticut, it was the housing boom after World War II that led to the economic design formula that makes the bathroom the 'meanest sized room in the house', at a standard 5ft x 7ft (1.5m x 2m). Builders wedged a standard 5ft (1.5m) bathtub

along one wall and this automatically became the standard measurement for two of the facing walls. Because the tub was 2½ft (76cm) wide, they squeezed the basin and lavatory into the remaining 4½ft (1.37m) on the wall at right angles to the tub. Ideally the lavatory would be in a separate area, but if this is not possible at least partially enclose it.

Grouping fixtures like the bath and shower together makes sense, or you could just combine the bath and shower head attachment. The good bathroom designer will install a pump booster with a shower so that you get a strong jet of water — some are so sophisticated that the water is aerated, giving a similar effect to pouring champagne over the head.

Apart from the main fixtures — bath, basin and lavatory — you will need somewhere to keep soap and toothbrushes, a place for shaving or putting on make-up, a dressing area, perhaps enough room to store towels or put in an airing cupboard. Bigger rooms could have space for exercising, a whirlpool jet tub, and a sofa or window seat as well as pictures and books, reminis-

The bathroom is often left out in the cold when people design their homes. It is enough for all the plumbing to work and bath, lavatory and basin to fit into the one tiny space. But what is functional can also be fun, and your bathroom can adopt many styles, from simple to sybaritic. In the two pictures, left and right, the same scene has been set in very different ways.
A mosaic of Victorian tiles has been used for an unusual splashplate (**left**). Although each tile has a different pattern, they are all the same size. If you would like to copy this idea with a collection of old tiles, make sure they are more or less the same size, or you will have some unsightly gaps in the mosaic. The marbled oval basin with walnut surround is Edwardian, as is the idea to panel the walls in wood. Edwardian bathrooms looked wonderfully luxurious and very manly with their glowing wood bath surrounds and paneled walls. Copy this idea with chipboard on the walls stained a walnut color, and decorated with picture frame molding. The lights are copies of Edwardian gas lights. The ferns on the edge of the bath and the pretty pitcher above the basin, add the final decorative flourishes.
Mirror glass has been set into wood surrounds (**right**) to create the maximum amount of light in this rather theatrical American bathroom. Note the light bulbs going down the side of the mirror over the oval sink: the idea was filched from theater dressing-rooms. Position the bulbs on either side of the mirror, as harsh light from above can 'bleach out' the reflection. Plain white tiles across the vanitory unit are an ideal background for treasured silver-topped scent bottles.

This loft bathroom (**left**), home of Dutch artist Ger Van Elk, explores the clinical style very successfully. Red and black border tiles and a turquoise tiled floor draw the eye to the pure architectural features. Note the dormer window which allows light to fall where it is most needed; over the corner bath.
Designer Adam Tihany has used mirror paneling (**above left**) to illusion of space in this tiny New York Furnetti apartment bathroom (**above left**). The handsome dark blue basins and bath are set into varnished wood surrounds.
White has been used everywhere in this bathroom cum-dressing-room (**above**), yet the effect is far from clinical. If the whole process of bathing proves too exhausting, then there's the Chevron quilted day-bed to recover on. The bath is actually hidden behind the white screen.

cent of David Hicks' designer bathrooms. However, larger bathrooms are not necessarily more luxurious than smaller ones. Often they are draughty, ill-lit, badly-carpeted, or sport acres of tiles that are cold underfoot. Heating and flooring are particular problems in large bathrooms.

Style

David Hockney's bathroom, featured in the film *A Bigger Splash*, can hardly be said to mark the turning point at which sanitaryware became high art, yet the bathroom was central to the theme, as in Hitchcock's *Psycho*. Tchaik Chassay, who designed the bathroom for David Hockney, is an architect who dislikes the fancy shapes and glittering finishes of fantasy bathrooms. He believes that fittings should be white, streamlined and classically shaped. He favors oval baths and semi-circular basins set in a custom-built top, with walls and floors covered with small square matt finish tiles in watery blues, grays and whites, to create a mosaic effect. He likes to put mirrors on the walls, and to cover double-fronted doors. He uses chrome fittings for cross-head taps and shower fit-

tings, and wall-mounted chrome Art Deco lights.

Bathroom designer Max Pike, who features a scarlet, roll-top, cast-iron bath in the window of his London showroom, says you can create an illusion of luxury with eye-catching fixtures, but nothing disguises the lack of well-designed fittings. Ideally, he likes white, or the creamy color, called Champagne. Max Pike enjoys working on exacting floor plans. He suggests grouping bath and basin to separate an area for the lavatory if you have a limited amount of space. Disguising the basin plumbing in a custom-built vanity unit offers extra storage space, as well as an opportunity for a paint finish such as dragging. Light grays, blues, white and minor finishes all add to the illusion of space.

An alternative to light colors and mirrored walls in a tiny, dark bathroom has been inspired by the grand, early twentieth-century cloakrooms with mahogany surrounds on white, cast-iron bathtubs and basins. The lavatory would be enclosed in a chair or box, like a commode, a design now manufactured commercially for smart washrooms. Chipboard paneling, stained mahogany, could cover the sides of

Why relegate your bathroom to a ting space, when it can perform so many useful functions. A bathroom can be the ideal dressing room, laundry room, exercise room, quiet reading room, or extended children's play area. Install speakers, and you can get the benefit of your stereo system while you soak. Line the walls with books, and soak up some good literature. A bathroom also makes a good photographic dark room, or even an excellent place for painting. Have a sofa or easy chairs instead of uncomfortable standard bathroom furniture, and members of the family can talk to you while you snuggle under the suds.

The bathroom (**left and inset**) is certainly spacious, and commands an excellent view of the London street below, yet is in no danger of being overlooked by curious neighbors. Superficially, it is a bathroom-cum-dressing room, but if you look hard at the dressing table by the window, you realize that it is in fact a solid mahogany desk. Just clear away the mirror, hair brushes and make-up, and you have the perfect spot for letter writing, novel writing, or crossword puzzle solving. Books jostle with after shave on the pine dresser (inset picture), and a special swivel mirror is exactly the right height for hair brushing. It is lit by a well-positioned downlight. The elegance of the bathtub is left unadorned for all to admire, exposed plumbing and all, but when your plumbing is as handsome as this, there is no need to be bashful. Less attractive pipe-work can always be painted in bright primary colors. The elegance of the bathtub is pure Edwardiana. these superb taps (**right**), made in brass from original Edwardian molds, come from the London firm of Czech and Speake. Mahogany paneling is used for the bath surround, and interior decorator Peter Farlow ragged the wall in an authentic dark clover color.

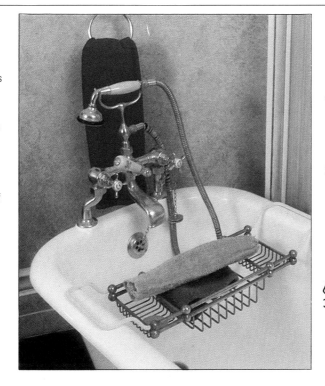

the bath and the walls to dado height, with smoky-brown tinted mirrors above. Cross-head brass taps and shower attachments, and a heated towel rack in brass would complete the setting.

Bath fittings assiduously ripped out of terrace houses and mansion blocks in the sixties, to be replaced with colored fiberglass, are now much sought after. Some specialist shops sell nothing but authentic and reproduction Victorian bath fittings — cast-iron baths, large square-topped pedestal basins, brass taps and mixers, wooden lavatory seats and 'finds' such as the four-poster bath with elaborate and lofty shower attachments on four corner pillars, similar to those in Manhattan hotels in the early twentieth century.

Rusty and stained old baths inherited with a house sometimes turn out to be beautiful Victorian porcelain enameled cast-iron baths. You can clean up the outside with a power drill fitted with a special wire brush attachment. When it is clean, paint it with rust inhibitor, primer and then a final coat of white gloss. The inside can be re-enameled by a professional resurfacing company, and rusty taps replaced with new ones to match the originals. One problem with free-standing cast-iron baths is that the plumbing always shows, for the shape prevents boxing in. To modern-

Bath and basin fittings can be highly decorative, but it is obviously important that they are chosen for practicality and you should check before you buy them that they can be comfortably turned and will be easy to clean when in place. Taps come in a huge variety of shapes and styles, to suit the most austere or cosy, stylized or luxurious bathroom scheme. The basic choice is between mixer taps providing a combined flow of hot and cold water or pillar taps giving separate supplies. Mixers may have two taps on either side of a swivel spout (**1**) or a fixed position spout (**3**). The fitments shown here also have a pop-up waste lever that controls emptying of the basin, perhaps a more elegant arrangement than the commonly seen chain-and-plug attachment. The single control basin mixer shown here (**2**) has a thickset, horizontal spout. This model operates by a lever control, turned one way for hot water, the other for cold, with graduating temperatures in between. A three-piece basin mixer (**4**) is similarly stoutly built, but the taps are mounted on either side of the spout and detached from it. Pillar taps (**5**) now have a streamlined, economical shape, but the old-fashioned types, originally of brass, are enjoying a new vogue. Their style has been adapted to a mixer design for a bath (**6**) with a broad central spout. New ideas again borrow from antique styling in ornate ceramic fitments (**7**). Taps are commonly finished in chrome, but you can choose more expensive gold-plated or antiqued silver or bronze finishes. Tap control knobs may or may not be an integral part of the unit; they range from clear or colored acrylic to polished onyx, or even the luxury of white marble, in simply sculptured or elaborately decorative designs.

The bathrooms on these pages make the most of limited space. There may not be extra room for installing an exercise bike or shelves of books, but the effect achieved by both designs is cool and uncluttered, almost aesthetic.

The Nordic influence has proved extraordinarily popular all over the world for bathroom schemes. The very sight of tongue-and-grooved pine clad walls is refreshing. English designer Alan Brown, who planned this bathroom (**left**) has used the Nordic style particularly expressively. The color scheme is basic, yet always successful: white pine and red. Bath and basin are plain white, as is the ceramic tiled floor and one wall. The other walls are pine clad, with large pieces of mirror glass inserted to double the apparant size of the room. Red is used for the 'extras': towels, mirror, lighting, and big plastic waste bin. The bathroom (**right**) shows how you can make an all white bathroom breathtakingly beautiful, and not at all clinical. Architect Bill Herman has an architect's preference for white sanitary ware, and he has built upon this basic colour scheme in a Manhattan apartment to create an exercise in purity and balance. Bits and pieces are carefully placed in a simple wicker basket, or hidden from view entirely in the pale maple cupboards beneath the double basin. Recessed spotlights in the ceiling, and a neon strip under the mirror in the basin alcove provide adequate and un-fussy lighting.

ists, this presents few problems, as they like to feature the plumbing as an integral part of the design, but those seeking a pretty bathroom will have to be inventive.

Designers Joan Barstow and Sandra Shaw canopied an old cast-iron claw-footed tub with fabric for the Philadelphia Vassar Club show-house. The high shower attachment inspired the chintz tent, which was draped around the bath and canopied into a shirred valance that hid the shower rod. Elastic in the hem tucked the edges neatly under the roll-top. The outside of the tub was then handpainted with a vine and flower design to repeat the pattern on the chintz.

The Nordic spa look is achieved very simply with white fittings, a corner bath or round tub, tongue-and-groove pine boarding on the ceiling and built

around pipes to conceal them. An exercise mat and bar on the walls for aerobics, and a touch of red on the taps, door handles and bath accessories will complete the healthy, energetic look.

A spectacular fantasy bathroom on the top floor of a New York residential block has an entire wall of reinforced glass, uncurtained because it is not overlooked, and commanding an unrivaled view of Manhattan as you step out of the wooden tub. This style of bathroom is dependent upon the site for its effect, yet more down-to-earth bathrooms can indulge flights of fancy with unusual fittings. Fantasists who wish to emerge Botticelli-like from a shell-shaped sunken bath can buy exotic fittings from Porcelaine de Paris, for example, or Bonsack. Hexagonal or shell-shaped baths can be sprigged with anemones, and

painted wisteria can adorn the bathtub, toilet, towelling, shower curtains and soap dishes. Tap heads can be decorated with a single flower, or you may prefer dolphin taps and turtle water spouts. American designer Sherle Wagner creates fantasy bathrooms with a waterlily set upon a pedestal stem, or a round basin lined with burnished pewter. Her specialty is painting flowers on basins with gloss paint, sealed with a watertight varnish: 'Chinese Cherry' or 'Wisteria' sprays in palest lilac blossom on white porcelain. The designer for the *James Bond* films actually borrows set pieces for bathrooms from 'West One', the bathroom shop in London. Finished in glittering gun-metal or black fox metallics and sunken into marble surrounds, with bolstered foam-filled head rests, these bathtubs are big enough to hold two or three bathers. However this range is not for anyone with limited space or funds.

Fabrics and paints in soft colors contribute to the pretty cottage freshness. Sue Leigh, former home editor on *Brides and Setting Up Home* magazine wanted a bathroom that had a light and airy country cottage style. When she bought her Victorian terrace house in London, the bath was in a small lean-to that also served as a kitchen. She decided to convert the bedroom above the kitchen, for easy water outlets, into a bathroom. The old cast-iron bath was renewed with professional enameling and set in the center of the room; a square pedestal basin from a demolition yard and a modern white toilet (the most expensive item) completed the fittings. The floorboards were sanded to a pale honey color and sealed, pale rugs in mint, white and rose were scattered on the floor, and the small fireplace — 'too pretty to rip out' — was painted inside with stove black and filled with ferns. Mint green and white wallpaper and matching tiles for the splashplate and hearth reinforced the color scheme, with ceiling, window frames and baseboards painted white. A fine chest of drawers housed towels, cotton wool, tissues, toilet paper, spare soaps and hot water bottles, and a set of open wicker shelves by the basin held toothbrushes, shaving gear, lotions, oils and shampoos. A bamboo bathrack accommodated washcloths, sponges, soap and a nail brush. 'Careful accessorizing contributes a lot to the final effect', says Sue Leigh. Hang prints and paintings, framed mirrors — not just a functional one over the basin — and put out a collection of sea shells and pebbles and a bowl of scented pot pourri.'

Repairing chipped basins with filler and painting designs with waterproof artists' oils is a good idea if

If you move into an old house and inherit sanitaryware dating back to the nineteenth century, don't even think about replacing it with acrylic modernity. The shapes of Victorian, Edwardian, even 1930s baths and sinks are enchanting, and they were constructed with pretty hard-wearing materials: glazed ceramic and cast-iron. You may even be lucky enough to inherit a decorated lavatory: all the rage one hundred years ago. Some such lavatory bowls are so intricately decorated, they are veritable works of art, attracting frantic bidding at auctions. By all means decorate an existing lavatory or basin, as has been skillfully done in this bathroom (**right**). Make sure first that the surface is properly enameled. Enamel can be renewed, either by yourself or by professionals. The pattern on this basin has been stenciled on and copied onto surrounding tiles.

The bathroom (**far left**) should satisfy the most glamorous bather. It has echoes of Edwardian decadence with its chandelier and flounced net curtains, and even earlier classical features, such as the marble floor and round sunken bath with Greek Key design Gold taps, and a finely decorated washbasin add the flourishes to a bathroom which may be a trifle excessive, but certainly fun.

The sunken bath (**left**) has a certain distinction. High above the American valleys a bather can watch the play of sunset or sunrise as the light filters through a delicate arrangement of windows and skylights. The tub can easily spring into life and become a jacuzzi and, for withstanding the sustained bliss of a scenic whirl, the tub has been specially contoured into seats and reclining positions. All in all, an idea to be treated carefully if you inhabit the northern hemisphere.

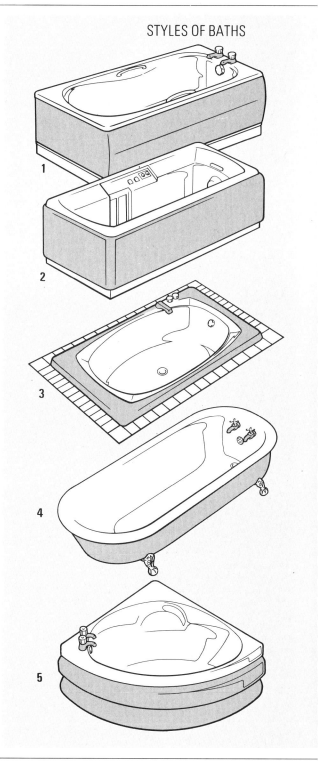

STYLES OF BATHS

The bathroom (**above**) not only doubles the apparent space with mirrors — but actually increases it ad infinitum. The Blumert residence in New York, designed by architects Ohrbach and Jacobson fairly glistens with reflected light, made dramatic by the chrome and black color scheme. The floor is constructed with black marble tiles and the same black marble has been laid across the white vanity unit. The walls are completely covered in mirror glass. The ceiling is metallic gray and the lighting consists of four gray downlighters, reflected forever in this dream world of mirrors. To anchor the color scheme, touches of scarlet have been used: on the monogramed towels, and the black and scarlet lacquered wicker containers. Notice the absence of clutter; the vanity unit is particularly well stocked with drawers and everything can be hideen from view.

STYLES OF BATHS

Whether your bathroom is cramped or generous, the bath can hardly go unnoticed, but with the range of fittings now available, you can choose whether to make it a dominant visual feature, or one that is simply functional, attractive but unobtrusive. Old-style, heavyweight baths were made from cast-iron with porcelain enameled finish. Modern baths are more likely to be pressed steel beneath the enameling: lightweight baths are formed from plastics. Plastics introduced an explosion of color to the cheaper ranges of bathroom fittings. White is still the least expensive choice, but delicate pastels are popular and higher priced designs include a range of vivid hues and rich, dark tones. To conceal awkward spaces or unsightly plumbing, you can buy preformed and coordinated panels; some are designed to include storage units within this otherwise wasted space. Standard baths now routinely incorporate features such as hand grips set in the sides and internal contouring designed to support the reclining body (**1**). Similar in design but different in effect is the bath that includes a whirlpool fitment (**2**). The system can be attached to any bath or you can select a specially designed model with this as its primary facility. A sunken bath (**3**) is often considered the height of luxury, but arrangements to fit and plumb it in must be carefully planned and costed. The old Victorian model of the free-standing bath is very much back in fashion (**4**). It need not be pressed against the wall; set it with the short side to the wall and allow it to protrude into the room, if you can successfully use the surrounding space. A corner bath (**5**) is space-saving; loss of length may be compensated by depth and comfort. Corner baths frequently include a recessed seat and can be adapted as shower units.

As a complete contrast to the picture on the opposite page, this charming vanity unit (**left**), has been built into an old pine dresser. Plumbing was no more difficult than plumbing a basin into a standard vanity/storage unit. If you like the look of old wood lovingly restored, polished and sealed, don't feel that you have to live without it in the bathroom and put up with shiny plastic. Hunt around junk shops for useful cupboards (old oak office furniture can be especially sturdy). As long as the wood is properly sealed, these pieces will make serviceable and attractive bathroom units.

you inherit old fittings in classic shapes. Designer Janet Allen of the Boston Junior League of Decorators spruced up a chipped basin with Renubath filler and then painted camellias over the basin base. When the oils had dried, she sealed the design with polyurethane to make it water resistant. Pipes situated below were concealed with the floral print fabric that inspired the camellia painting, and this was gathered into a shirred smocking top.

Plumbing

Few things are as irritating as showers that trickle, and baths that drain slowly. Good plumbing (and that means easy access to both inlet and outlet pipes) is essential. Make a plan of where the water supply and waste pipes enter, and make a layout that uses existing plumbing. Mandatory regulations concern waste water, which must flow into the down pipe on the ex-

terior wall. If fittings are positioned at a distance from this pipe, you may need to raise the floor area to get a good angle for swift drainage.

Baths

The standard American bath is rectangular, measuring about 67in x 30in (170cm x 76cm). Slightly narrower baths are available, but they are rarely less than 26½in (67cm) wide. Cast-iron tubs from Europe are sometimes 47in (120cm) long and slightly deeper for soaking; the "Sitty" from Italy measures 47in x 29½in (120cm x 75cm) and has deep sides and a shaped base for comfort.

Corner baths make better use of floor space than rectangular models, but make sure they will fit through door and stair space if you install them upstairs. The corner bath or shower is even deeper and supplied with a curved shower rail. Oriental soaking

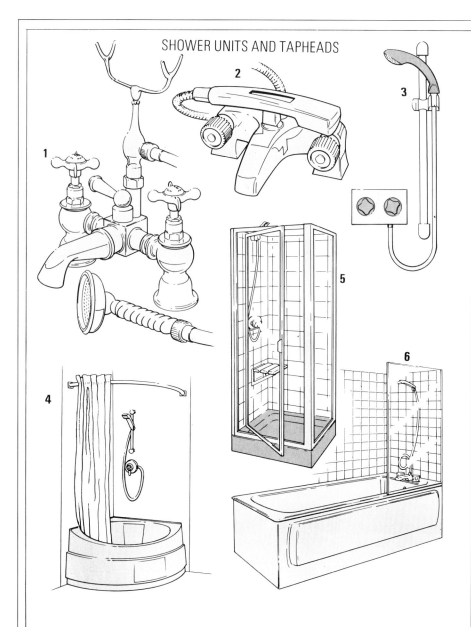

SHOWER UNITS AND TAPHEADS

A shower spray fitted to bath taps is handy for hair-washing or a quick all-over wash. Such fittings come in a variety of styles — imitating the old Edwardian brass taps (**1**) or from streamlined modern ranges of chrome and acrylic fittings (**2**). A neat and economical wall unit (**3**) can be installed above the bath or in a separate space with shower tray and curtains. Showers spread steam and condensation, so be sure to check damp-proofing of walls. A corner bath can be adapted to include a shower (**4**), closed off with a curtain on a specially designed curving rail. For luxury and complete privacy, erect a self-contained shower cubicle (**5**), with rigid plastic walls and a plastic or enameled-metal shower tray. Such units can be placed outside the bathroom — in a hall or bedroom alcove, for example — if plumbing arrangements permit. Alternatively, for a spray attachment wall-mounted above the bath, use plastic panels to enclose the space (**6**). If the side flap is hinged, it can be pushed back against the wall when not in use.

tubs combine the sit-down bath with a shower in a space not much larger than a shower tray. Lowering the bath effectively increases the apparent size of the bathroom, though it is a job for the professionals. A sunken bath can make even the smallest bathroom look luxurious and the best bathroom shops feature several.

Some baths also provide room for storage, like the Armitage Shanks bath with a side panel that can be let down to reveal space for bottles, cleaning fluids and more practical bathroom accessories. American designer Patricia Drummond placed a simple but solid wooden frame over a functional bathtub, topped it with a platform and added upholstered cushions, pillows and a curtain to turn it into a seating alcove by day.

Whirlpool baths make bathing a health spa exercise; they are invigorating and increasingly recognized as beneficial to stress. The first model was invented by Senor Jacuzzi for his arthritic son. Today whirlpool baths have many different names, but they all operate on the same principle: strategically placed jets regulate the pummeling or swirling effect of the water. Some maternity homes install Jacuzzis to help in the first stages of labor. As long as your ceiling joists can support the weight of a Jacuzzi it is a feasible alternative to several weeks on a health farm where they are used to help break down excessive cellulite.

Showers

Manufactured shower cubicles that separate the shower from the bath area are complete units made of metal, plastic sheets or glass fiber, with all the fittings and attachments. They are completely waterproof and need only to be connected to the water supply and waste pipes. Thermostatically-controlled fittings for the shower ensure that the water is at the correct temperature. The head of the shower has to be at least 3ft (91cm) below the bottom of the cold water tank for adequate water pressure, though electric pumps can give booster pressure.

Basins

Usually rather wide and deep, the smallest basin measures 20in x 16in (51cm x 40.5cm). In a single-bathroom house it is worth installing the largest basin you can buy. Decorator Diana Phipps recommends fitting kitchen-sink faucets as they have a longer spout than the standard bathroom version, and make hair washing more pleasant. A wall-mounted basin means exposed plumbing, so build in a narrow shelf to par-

The bathroom (**left**) belongs to Frans Molenaar, the dress designer, and was designed by Mark Sutton-Vane. White is the dominant theme, and it has been used for the sanitary-ware, for the tiles, paintwork and curtains. Floor, walls, and bath and basin surrounds are tiled, yet strangely, the effect is not clinical and austere, but very pretty, and the little round basin looks quite endearing.

TYPES OF BASINS

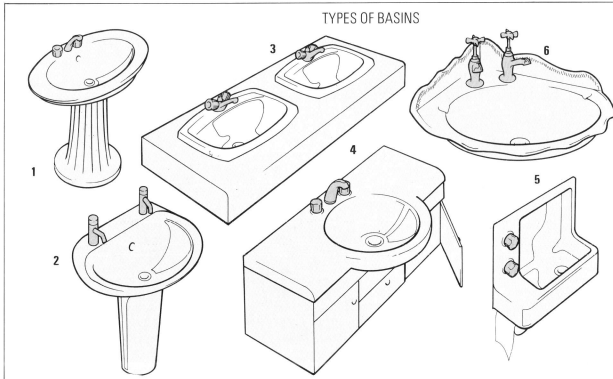

Basins are made from a variety of materials, including vitreous china, enameled steel or lightweight plastics. Like baths, they are available in a wide range of colours and styles. Pedestal designs include a sturdy, old-style basin with fluted column (**1**) or a simple, modern shape with clean lines, a generous bowl and a flat back to fit snugly to the wall (**2**). More lavish with space are built-in basins — the double vanity unit (**3**) sunk into a laminated counter top, which can be backed with a sweep of mirrors, or a moulded fitment with a built-in base which provides extra storage space (**4**). An advantage of built-in basins is that they conceal plumbing completely. An economical design that can be suitably fitted beside the toilet is a shallow basin partly recessed into the wall (**5**). A corner basin can save space in the bathroom, even if it is elaborately styled with shell-like edges and old fashioned taps (**6**). A wall-hung basin should be fixed securely to a load-bearing wall.

PLANNING A BATHROOM

700mm

1100mm

700mm

750-900mm

1000mm

700mm

600mm

800mm

800mm

600mm

An important factor often overlooked in bathroom planning is the full amount of space required for each of the fittings, not only to accommodate the appliance itself, but also to ensure safe, comfortable use and easy movement from one unit to the next. The diagrams (**above**) show the ideal user space for the bath, shower, basin, toilet and bidet. As shown in the bathroom floor plan (**top right**), the space can be allowed to overlap.

tially conceal pipes, or cover with tongue-and-groove boarding on battens. A dual-purpose solution to this problem is to build a cupboard under a wall-mounted basin to hide the pipes and provide storage space. If you are paneling the wall to cover the basin plumbing and house the lavatory cistern as well, make sure the height of the cistern lines up with the height of the basin. You can always consider a pedestal basin instead of a wall-mounted one as it will leave more floor space.

Bathroom accessories
Most people associate yards of mirror with luxurious bathrooms. Mirrors certainly create the illusion of space, but they need a lot of cleaning and can throw back reflections that are not visually appealing. If you do favor mirrors, consider the slightly tinted ones in bronze tones for a healthy glow. If your walls are plasterboard, buy featherlight mirrors made of plastic film on polythene sheets, coated with aluminum, which need no structural support and are less inclined to steam up.

Put up open shelving to hold your prettier bottles

What in America is called the 'master bath' and in England the main or the ensuite bathroom, is more and more being geared to relaxation, and not just to puritan cleansing and unenjoyable showering down.

The bathroom (**above**), located in a French château, is just such a relaxing spot. It is a very elegant, pannelled, ensuite bathroom with its tie-back curtains and period furniture. In fact it can be used just as well as a dressing room, as it can a bathroom; the large bay window, an unusual feature in a bathroom, allows plenty of natural light for applying make-up.

The bathroom (**right**) is a neat ensuite, making good use of a space created by an alcove. A simple foot tub doubles as a shower, and the white tiles are nicely decorated with splashes of red.

and jars. Pick a good background color for the shelves and place a few items on them, such as coral or shells, or buy boldly colored towels to accent it. Thus a deep blue shelf can be emphasized with lavender and turquoise towels in a white bathroom.

Heated brass or chome towel racks that are timed to warm up an hour before bathtime are cost effective and provide cosiness in winter. Hang hooks for towels at lower levels for small children, as it is easier for them to hang towels on pegs than over bars.

Windows
Blinds make the most practical window dressing in the bathroom, unless you have a large bathroom that will take drapes. You can improve split bamboo blinds with yellow-ocher paint, thinned down with turpentine, and a coat of French polish.

Walls
If you inherit large, square glazed tiles in a rather sludgy color, take off the top third and paint the wall surface a matching color in gloss paint for shine, putting on several coats for a deeper tone. Then stencil a border pattern along the wall-to-ceiling edge, and paint a simple pattern on the tiles. You could paint a ribbon design, threaded through each tile with mock eyelets. Shade the bottom for emphasis and on every sixth tile, paint a bow in the middle. A pastel striped cotton dhurrie rug on the floor will link the colors beautifully.

Floors
Foam-backed tumbletwist, used to cover bedroom

Both the bathrooms on these pages are typically small in size, yet the treatment is radically different. The bathroom and small picture inset (**left**) is fresh and pretty, Mediterranean-fashion, in crunchy blues and sweet pinks. The bathroom (**right**) has a kind of outrageous adolescent charm which harks back to the confident swinging sixties. Neither high-tech, nor minimalist, it is quite simply rebelious with its white vinyl padded walls, black painted shelving unit, and black door. The architect is Jan Kapilchy who wanted a tiny bathroom in a tiny London apartment to look that bit different.

Joss and Daphne Graham designed the bathroom (**left**) for their London home. They were clever enough to match blue and white tiles from Portugal, with crisp wallpaper and matching border from Osborne and Little and with Colefax and Fowler chintz for the festoon blind. Daphne Graham maintains that ordinary curtains are a nuisance in a bathroom, yet a festoon blind, especially in chintz, and with a pleated taffeta edging adds a touch of flamboyance. Notice how the wallpaper border starts at the top of the window, and not where the ceiling meets the walls. This is quite deliberate. As Daphne explains: 'The idea of a border at this level was to visually take the ceiling downwards as the room is taller than it is wide.'. Above the bath is a rather lovely Japanese painting of a fish on silk. The rag rug is Swedish, and the custom built unit around the basin has been dragged with cream over white, and the molded edge scumbled with blue.

TYPES OF TOILETS

The basic components of a toilet suite — bowl, seat and cistern — may be bought as an integrated unit (**right**) or chosen separately. The bowl and pedestal are likely to be made of vitreous china, in a range of colors and styles to match other bathroom fittings, and the cistern of plastic or china. Plastic toilet seats have become standard, being lightweight, easy to clean and inexpensive, but wooden seats are also available. A bidet accompanying the toilet may be conveniently styled, with pillar taps or a mixer tap unit only, or may include more sophisticated features, such as a flushing rim or water supply in the form of an ascending spray.

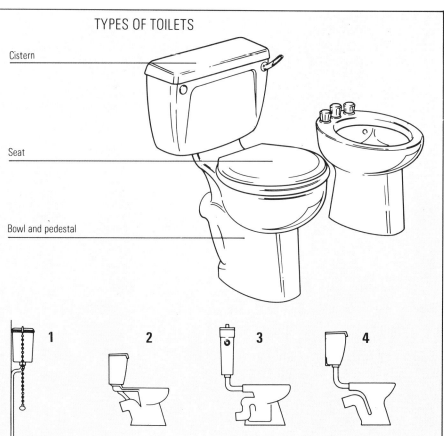

Cistern

Seat

Bowl and pedestal

Toilet waste disposal works by a wash-down flow of water or by syphonic action which drains the bowl from below. A cistern may be mounted at high level (**1**) with a chain pull or above and behind the bowl (**4**) with a flush-control lever. More economical of space are the close-coupled suite (**2**) or the slimline cistern (**3**). The cistern is concealed behind the bowl in a ducted unit with removable panel (**5**) or behind a false wall for use with a cantilevered bowl bracketed into wall and floor (**6**).

1   2   3   4

5   6

floors, is also practical for the bathroom, although it is rather bulky. Smoother foam-backed vinyls and ceramic tiles are preferred for the eighties bathroom. Chipboard floor tiles that are sealed with polyurethane make a warm base underfoot and are the cheapest solution for a large area. The most expensive floor covering is wall-to-wall carpeting, preferably in nylon or acrylic, as these materials dry out more quickly than wool.

Lighting

Electricity and water don't mix, but fortunately safety regulations governing the placing of electrical sockets in bathrooms make wearing rubber boots to change a light bulb merely an unnecessary precaution. Accord-ing to American standards, the only socket allowed in a bathroom is for an electric razor, on a low wattage. Mirror lights often incorporate shaver sockets with an isolating transformer to minimalize any shock. Light switches have to be placed outside the bathroom door, although you can have a pull-cord switch inside the bathroom. Bathroom light fittings are usually fairly restrained, with a ceiling-mounted overhead light and task lighting at the mirror.

To ensure an adequate amount of light, remember that filament lighting needs 20 watts per square meter, and fluorescent lighting needs 10 watts. Thus a bathroom measuring 6½ft x 9¾ft (2m x 3m) requires 120 watts of filament lighting, which could be planned as an overhead light of 60 to 80 watts with additional

Fiona Skrine created the unique, delicate decoration for this small bathroom by the simple stenciling process shown here.

1. Draw out the motifs for the design on tracing paper, using a soft, dark pencil.

2. Transfer the motifs to stencil film and go over them to mark the outlines clearly. Transparent film enables you to see the layout of motifs underneath as you apply the paint.

3. With a fine, sharp scalpel, cut carefully around the outlines.

4. Place the stencil firmly on the surface and fill the shape with color. Use a flat-ended stenciling brush with stiff bristle and keep the paint to a fairly dry consistency.

5. Repeat the process with different shapes and colors until the design is complete. Then shell the surface with varnish or a solution of PVA, which is white while liquid but dries to a clear, waterproof finish.

1

2

3

4

5

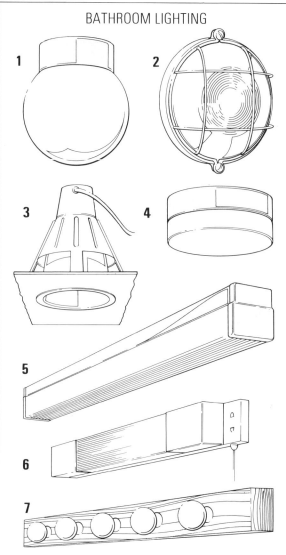

BATHROOM LIGHTING

There is almost nothing more essential to the enjoyment of a decent bath than a properly warmed towel. No such problem arises in the bathroom above. A ceiling high towel rail by the Swiss company Zehnder could keep a newly bathed rugby team happy with dry towels. The sink has been recessed into an alcove, amply lit by a wall of frosted glass, divided by bright green bars.

small wattage above the mirror. Diffused light could be given from wall-mounted fittings. Chrome and white glass Art Deco lights look good in a bathroom with matt finish white and gray tiles, chrome or nickel taps and lots of mirrors.

For shadow-free illumination, make sure the light is directed at the face rather than at the mirror. Actors and actresses fringe their makeup mirrors with a ring of light bulbs, a trick copied by bathroom manufacturers, but regrettably often with bulbs only along the top. This has the same effect on the eyes as badly positioned downlights, so hang the mirror upside down

Bathroom lighting must combine efficiency and safety, as well as adding something to the mood of a well-designed room. For a general source, enclosed ceiling lights come in a variety of styles: a globe (**1**) or cylinder (**4**) or the bulk head lamp with wire grille which can be ceiling or wall mounted (**2**)or the fully-recessed downlighter (**3**). Fluorescent strip lighting is a powerful source, pleasantly dispersed by a diffuser cover (**5**). A

small striplight (**6**) for a basin mirror is fitted with a shaver socket; the socket has a built-in safety device and is the only type allowed in a bathroom. The theatrical style of a row of bulbs is an attractive idea for task lighting, mounted in a simple pine strip (**7**). See also Lighting, pages 50-53.

The bathroom (**left**) is in the Klein apartment, designed by the Space Design Group. Gray is the predominant color, both on the tiled floor, and the tiled walls. The bath is on a platform, which actually creates more space for lounging, and undressing, than a normal floor-level bath. A row of theatrical spotlights illuminates the mirror and sink area, and the shelving and storage systems are all glass, for easy visability.

The bathroom (**below**) is high tech at its jolliest, and least serious. Exposed pipework has been painted in child's crayon box colors. contrasting with the clinical white tiling. Jokey lights on mock pipe work stands peer into the room's interior.

so that the light travels upward. Cheaper everyday bathroom light fittings are bulk-head lights to match wire grid soap dishes and bath accessories. Fun lights for bathrooms include a fluorescent tube captured in a Mickey Mouse gloved hand attached to the wall, and a light bulb in a pickling jar, suspended from a twirly cord.

Heating and ventilation

Bathrooms must be warm. An appliance that creates instant heat is all that is needed, provided it complies with the stringent safety regulations. No socket outlets may be installed, apart from the shaver socket, so electric heaters and towel racks must be permanently fixed and connected directly to the circuit wiring by an electrician. Wall-mounted heaters with safety pull cords are sometimes combined with light fittings for the center of the ceiling. Other models can be adjusted to beam warmth where it is most needed.

According to building regulations, any internal bathroom (one without access to fresh air), is obliged to have an extractor fan that comes on automatically with the light switch. Extractor fans fitted to the wall (or in the window) will provide the efficient solution to any ventilation problems in the bathroom.

AWKWARD SPACES

The current trend for redesigning space in contemporary houses has resulted in the imaginative transformation of awkward space into extra space for accommodating hobbies, books, countertops and equipment. Older houses that have an attic or basement are considered good value as these areas can be readily converted, but even streamlined modern blocks have corridors, landings and space under stairs.

In the past decade the basement has graduated from the junk room to the more functional work center. An adequate damp-proof course and the installation of a solid fuel or wood-burning stove with a central flue (warmth travels upwards so it will heat the rest of the house), make the area habitable. Use all available sources of natural light and install window seats with hinged lids for storing clutter. In the evening use a back-up system of directional lamps and clamp-on movable lights.

The basement also provides generous floor space for a large table, so essential to the model-maker, train-set enthusiast or seamstress. A trestle table makes a good cutting surface in a basement that converts to a sewing room, with a separate lower table for the machine, cupboards with wide shelves for folded cloth, deep drawers for patterns, shallow drawers for pins, scissors, silks, chalks and tapes, a full-length mirror, a fold-out ironing board and perhaps a small sink for damp pressing. Practical vinyl flooring is best for a work area as it can be cleaned easily.

The basement, attic or hall will invariably have stairs leading to it. Convert the space under the stairs into a cupboard by putting panels over the meter and fuse boxes and adding a strip light ('cool' lighting that will not overheat). Here you can store cleaning equipment — fluids, mops and brooms — on shelving, clips and hooks. For electrical equipment such as vacuum cleaners, run the basement or hall flooring surface into the cupboard so that you can maneuver the appliances on an even surface. A more unusual yet practical idea for storing household tools is to fit a pull-out box on castors under the first tread of the staircase. Turn the area below stairs into a more interesting arrangement than merely a site for cleaning materials, by filling the space with a bed covered in a striped weave that complements the stair carpet and painting the bannisters in alternating colors.

Open-tread stairs make very good shelves if extended along the wall. Continue the line of the first tread into a narrow shelf that runs along the wall, providing space for an ar-

Making the most of the nooks and crannies in your home can become something of an enthusiasm for the ergonomically minded apartment or house dweller; but for those people who are so pressed for space they feel that their homes are squeezing them out, ingenious invention becomes a necessity.

The tiny London mews apartment (**left**) was completely gutted by its architect owner to create more usable space. This neat little dining area fits into the narrow space at the top of the staircase. While dining, guests can enjoy peering down into the hallway below as well as enjoying the more interesting vista of a roof garden open to the stairs at the top of the spiral staircase.

An awkward corner (**right**) has become a neat kitchen with refrigerator, sink and storage space all crammed into a very small area, and painted bright green for instant jollity.

LOFT CONVERSIONS

There is no doubt that it is less expensive and in many instances preferable, to utilize space in your home rather than move to a larger place. If you are lucky enough to have a good-sized loft investigate the possibility of using it or converting it to give you an extra area. This could prove to be the most pleasant and popular room in the house.

There are endless possibilities: you could have an open-plan scheme or divide the space into a work area (lofts make wonderful studios), spare room, bedroom or play room You could even open the loft to the floor below to make a high-ceilinged room with rafters. By adding a platform for bedding or seating, you would be making good use of the existing loft.

Before you proceed with your plan for conversion, consider such things as structural alterations; stair access and the laws governing this; weatherproofing; adequate light from windows and skylights; flooring and storage. Remember also that a loft will be very warm in

summer so you will need some protection from solar heat. You can use blinds inside or weatherproofed pinoleum blinds fixed on the outside, but operated from the inside.

Insulation As long as the roof is adequately insulated there should

be no problem keeping the loft warm in winter as heat will rise from the rest of the house. Consult an expert on the type of roof insulation to use. If the water tank is above the roof you will have to box it separately.

Flooring Most loft floors were originally considered as ceilings for the floor below, so make quite sure that they are strong enough to take additional weight. Floorboards can be stripped and polished, or painted and covered with rugs or carpeted to provide extra soundproofing.

Storage Traditionally used for storing junk, lofts have many nooks and crannies that can be utilized in a functional room. Sloping roofs provide excellent storage space in a loft and are often good places to put the bed, chest, cupboards or shelves. From the preceding page we have followed the spiral staircase up to the loft of this tiny London mews flat. It is in fact not a loft in the conventional sense at all, because the roof flips open to reveal a roof garden in questionable taste! Squares of astro-turf line the floor and a bright red frame covered with canvas provides shade, and variable shelter should it rain. Class side walls ensure that the rest of the house benefits fully from the light and sense of aerial space.

rangement of objects, or extend one tread width to make a desk, using the treads above the desk as bookshelves.

For the wine collector, this area could be an ideal place to set up a cellar. You should be able to stack a dozen bottles of wine to rib height (approximately six treads deep) with nine bottles across the width of the staircase. Above the wine rack, add a narrow shelf for jars of olives, nuts and other accompaniments.

Spiral staircases in small townhouses take up less space than a conventional staircase and can be enlivened with paint, in a bold color. Use a wallpaper with a vertical stripe to accentuate the curvy height of the staircase. Landings midway along a conventional staircase need not be wasted space. Obviously the size of the landing dictates how you use it, but on a large landing you can set up a desk below a window to create a simple study.

Stair carpet
Wall-to-wall carpeting that is suitable in weight and texture for the stairs is very expensive, although it

has the advantage of sound-proofing the treads. The cheapest heavy-duty carpets are haircords and needle-looms: rush matting is also cheap but more difficult to lay. Try painting the stairs and running a heavy-duty sisal matting up the center. Traditional carpet strips are only 27in (68.5cm) so the border trims on either side of the carpet must be sanded and sealed.

Many staircases are made of hardwood which can be sealed and polished. Sanded floorboards can be stained with a white emulsion, watered down thinly to take the dappled gray/white paint wash. Or paint stairs with four coats of a matt black varnish after sanding, applying a final coat of varnish before you leave for your vacation, as it takes some time to dry.

Halls
The first impression of your house is given by the hall. Sadly it is often the area that is most neglected because it has no specific function, other than to serve as the reception area for letters and visitors.

The size and shape of the hall usually makes it an awkward place to decorate. Often it houses the pipes

This American family home (**above**) has a multi-functional loft area. Arranged on various levels, the loft areas are either fully open to the skies, partially covered, or proper enclosed room. In this loft the bedroom leads out to a semi-enclosed patio and a bathroom. Further on a wide and sunny balcony houses a round warm tub for outdoor bathing.

The tiny kitchen (**right**) is cleverly tucked away behind louvered doors that can fold across in a flash to hide the clutter.

and the meter points, in addition to being the darkest place in the whole house. One advantage is that you can decorate it as dramatically as you like, introducing decorating ideas that you might be reluctant to try in a larger area. In a large hallway, use the black and white diamond-patterned flooring made of cushion-backed vinyl which imitates a grand tiled entrance.

The hall is a perfect place for displaying your enthusiasms. So boots and oilskins suggest the great outdoors, while sun hats and pannier baskets, together with botanical prints, indicate a keen interest in gardening. If you are a winter sport enthusiast you could decorate the hallway with photographs of snowy peaks and hang skis on the sloping wall of the stairwell. A perch mounted in a glass case, a green net on the wall, some rods and a picnic hamper make a decorative set-piece at the same time as accommodating the angler's equipment.

In a modern townhouse that has few architectural features, a dado rail running around the hall area and up the stairs can suggest an alternative paint color. Either hand-marble or use marbled wallpaper below the dado line, with a lighter color taking the eye upward. A group of pictures, a table set with some flowers and an elegant mirror will make this a gracious reception area. In a nineteenth-century house you can make full use of a generously proportioned entrance hall by decorating it with flocked wallpaper in an elaborate floral pattern, painting the door in high gloss, and using curtains on rails to conceal adjoining doors.

If you have used patterned wallpaper in the living room, decorate the hall with a sympathetic scheme. An oriental woven carpet, for example, is complemented by a hall in red lacquer paint with a pair of blue and white ginger jars forming the umbrella stand. For a style that contrasts textures, linking exterior finish to interior simplicity, make a feature of unplastered walls, a wooden tongue-and-groove ceiling, tiled flooring in cork or vinyl, and an array of plants chosen for their foliage.

Since the hall is usually a small area, you can try out an elaborate wallcovering which would be too expensive to use over a larger surface area. This makes it the ideal place to experiment with fabric on walls. A lightweight dress fabric, such as striped shirting, can be glued directly on to the wall; polyester wadding underneath will make it more luxurious. Border it with a woven webbing strip or ribbon to hide ragged edges at the top and bottom. Hang a central light, add

a console table (with flowers), a few formal pictures.

Wallpaper paneling can create a wonderful landscape in an entrance hall. Open up a romantic vista with instant *trompe l'oeil* on a grand scale, showing balustrades and urns on a terrace by the sea, mysterious castles or follies, or a naïve jungle painting.

In a long corridor hallway, make use of the corridor aspect by turning the space into a library. Bookshelves give the peaceful feeling of browsing in a library. Take the shelves up as high as possible and add a tortoiseshell or bamboo ladder to heighten the effect. Mirror paneling can also look good, set opposite fanlights or doorways so that light bounces back into the dark hallway, but place them discreetly as it can be disconcerting for guests to see mirror images of themselves as they enter unfamiliar surroundings. Another idea is to create a little gallery for drawings, prints or miniatures. Avoid hanging a large painting in a small hallway as you need to be about 12ft (3.6m) away in order to view it properly. Ceiling spots or downlights that bathe the walls in light are good in halls, and deep, vibrant colors such as red, brown, peach or coral will make a drafty hall warmer and more intimate without reducing its size. A highly glazed ceiling that reflects light on its surfaces will give a feeling of space.

A built-in wardrobe has been converted into a dressing table alcove simply by removing the wardrobe doors (**far left**). The door frames have been painted brilliant red, and the interior of the alcove has been papered in a pretty pink design to match the pink walls of the rest of the room. Dried flowers hang from the original top shelf of the wardrobe, and a simple Victorian mahogany mirror sits on the lower shelf.

A high-tech steel mesh trolley on castors serves as a drinks table and magazine rack and can be moved to anywhere in the room.

A space-age cubicle (coveniently marked with a K) is the kitchen in this living room-cum-kitchen/diner (**left**). Inside the aircraft like step over door is a fully fitted kitchen with enough storage space and appliances squeezed into a tiny space to keep anybody happy and well fed.

Careful planning is the key to decorating success; prepare a checklist of all stages in the work, such as applying sealer, undercoat or lining paper, as well as the work involved in putting on the final surface. It is important to calculate quantities as accurately as possible before buying paint, wallpaper, fabric or tiles, but it is best to err on the generous side, as it can be difficult to match a precise shade or pattern. Make sure you have items such as adhesives, dilutents and solvents suited to the task and the materials.

Paint Different types of paint have different covering power, and this is further affected by the condition of the surface being painted — rough or porous walls use up more paint. Multiply height by width of the walls to find the basic area to be covered and refer to the paint chart (right). If mixing your own tint, work out the proportions of each color using small sample cans and then translate the ratio into larger quantities. Remember to calculate the ceiling area also, if necessary, or make a separate estimate.

Wallpapers The width and length of a roll of wallpaper depends upon its origin. American and European papers are usually 18in (0.46m) wide, but in length are 8yds (7.35m) and 9yds (8.25m) respectively. Standard English sizing is 21in (0.53m) width by 11yds (10.05m) length. The charts (far right) show how to calculate the number of rolls, based on these measurements, according to the height of the walls and the measurement right around the room. To match a large repeat pattern accurately at the seams, you will need to allow for wastage.

Fabrics For a wall-covering, it is easiest to use paper-backed fabrics which behave like wallpaper. Unbacked fabrics are difficult unless specially treated and must be overlapped when hung, meaning wastage on each width. To calculate fabric for curtains, multiply the length of curtain track by the fullness recommended for the heading tape, divide it by the fabric width to find the number of widths needed, and multiply this figure by the drop, allowing for hems and matching patterns at the seams.

Tiles Tiles are available in an increasing variety of shapes and sizes and again it is better to overestimate slightly (see chart far right). It is almost impossible to fit tiles precisely to a given area, so arrange them to have cut sections at the bottom of the wall or tucked away in a corner.

Adhesives There are a number of specialized brand-name adhesives for particular decorating jobs. These may be recommended by the manufacturer or supplier of tiles, wallpaper and wall fabrics, but there are also three basic types of adhesive that cover different needs. It is easier to bond two materials of basically similar composition than to join two quite different substances. The strongest bond is provided by epoxy resin adhesives; these are two-part components that must be mixed freshly for each time of using. The resin takes about six hours to set. Less tough, but also useful for decorating are contact adhesives; the glue is spread on both surfaces and allowed to become tacky before they are pressed together. Clear household adhesives are valuable for small repairs. Other types are increasingly in use — PVA for wood and plastics or rubber latex for carpet and fabric repairs. If in doubt about the adhesive needed for your job, take advice from a reliable DIY supplier.

PAINT: AMOUNTS

Quantity	Emulsion		Gloss	
	sq yds	(sq m)	sq yds	(sq m)
1 pint (0.568 litres)	12	(10)	10	(8½)
1 quart (1.135 litres)	24	(20)	20	(17)
1 gallon (4.54 litres)	96	(80)	80	(67)

PAINT: INTERIOR USES

Ceilings and Walls

Water paint:	flat finish (2 coats), not washable, thin with water
*Oil-bound distemper:	Flat finish (2 coats), not washable, thin with water
Emulsion paint:	flat or semi-gloss finish (2 coats), washable, cheap, but use in high condensation areas not recommended
Oil paint:	high gloss, semi-gloss or flat finish (2 coats), washable, thin with turpentine

Woodwork

Emulsion paint:	flat or semi-gloss finish (2 coats), thin with water, do not use as an undercoat for oil paints
Oil paint:	high gloss, semi-gloss or flat finish (2 coats), easily cleaned
Plastic paints:	high gloss finish (1 or 2 coats), do not thin, quick-drying, non-drip

Iron or Steel

Oil paint:	gloss or semi-gloss finish (2 coats), use alkali-resistant primer, thin with turpentine
Plastic paints:	high gloss finish (1 or 2 coats), do not thin, quick-drying, non-drip

Lead, copper, zinc

Oil Paint:	gloss or semi-gloss finish (2 coats), use wire wool and white spirit to clean the surface, use special primer, thin with turpentine

AMERICAN WALLPAPERS

Ft/m around room	Height of wall (ft/m)		
	8ft (2.4m)	9ft (2.7m)	10ft (3.0m)
28 (8.5)	7	8	9
32 (9.6)	8	9	10
36 (11)	9	10	11
40 (12.2)	10	11	12
44 (13.4)	11	12	14
48 (14.6)	12	13	15
52 (15.8)	13	15	16
56 (17.0)	14	16	17
60 (18.3)	15	17	19
64 (19.5)	16	18	20
68 (20.7)	17	19	21
72 (21.9)	18	20	22
76 (23.2)	19	21	24
80 (24.4)	20	22	25
84 (25.6)	21	23	26
88 (26.8)	22	24	27

ENGLISH WALLPAPERS

Ft/m around room	Height of wall (ft/m)		
	8ft (2.4m)	9ft (2.7m)	10ft (3.0m)
28 (8.5)	4	5	6
32 (9.6)	5	6	7
36 (11)	6	6	7
40 (12.2)	7	7	8
44 (13.4)	7	8	8
48 (14.6)	8	8	9
52 (15.8)	8	9	10
56 (17.0)	9	9	10
60 (18:3)	9	10	11
64 (19.5)	10	10	12
68 (20.7)	10	11	13
72 (21.9)	11	12	13
76 (23.2)	12	12	14
80 (24.4)	12	13	15
84 (25.6)	13	14	16
88 (26.8)	14	14	16

The charts on this page will help you to estimate the number of rolls/tiles you need. The larger the pattern, the more paper you need to allow for matching. You also need to allow for more tiles if they are not square. Always ask your retailer's advice.

To calculate the number of rolls required for ceilings using imperial measurements, work out the square area in yards and divide by four. To calculate the number of rolls with metric measurements, work out the square area in meters and divide by five.

CONTINENTAL WALLPAPERS

Ft/m around room	Height of wall (ft/m)		
	8ft (2.4m)	9ft (2.7m)	10ft (3.0m)
28 (8.5)	6	7	7
32 (9.6)	7	8	8
36 (11)	8	8	9
40 (12.2)	8	9	10
44 (13.4)	9	10	11
48 (14.6)	10	11	12
52 (15.8)	11	12	13
56 (17.0)	12	13	14
60 (18.3)	12	14	15
64 (19.5)	13	15	16
68 (20.7)	14	16	17
72 (21.9)	15	16	18
76 (23.2)	16	18	20
80 (24.4)	17	19	21
84 (25.6)	18	20	22
88 (26.8)	19	21	23

TILES

Sq. ft. (sq m)	4in × 4in (10cm × 10cm)	6in × 6in (15cm × 15cm)	8in × 8in (20cm × 20cm)
2 (.19)	18	8	5
4 (.37)	36	16	9
6 (.56)	54	24	14
8 (.74)	72	32	18
10 (.93)	90	40	23
12 (1.11)	108	48	27
14 (1.30)	126	56	32
16 (1.49)	144	64	36
18 (1.67)	162	72	41
20 (1.86)	180	80	45
22 (2.04)	198	88	50
24 (2.23)	216	96	54

DIRECTORY OF SOURCES

This directory includes addresses of some of the many firms, manufacturers and designers referred to in the book.

USEFUL ADDRESSES

National Gas Consumer's Council
162 Regent St
London W1R 5TB

Electricity Council
30 Millbank
London SW1

Solid Fuel Advisory Service
Hobart House
Grosvenor Place
London SW1X 7AE

Microwave Oven Association
16a The Broadway
London SW19
supplies information and literature on different types of ovens.

The Design Council
28 Haymarket
London SW1Y 4SU

National Trust Collection
36 Queen Anne's Gate
London SW1H 9AS

FABRICS/WALLPAPERS

Cole & Son
PO Box 4BU
18 Mortimer St
London W1A LBU

Conran
The Conran Shop
77-79 Fulham Road
London SW3

G P & J Baker
18 Berners St
London W1

Souleiado
171 Fulham Road
London SW3

John Oliver
33 Pembridge Road
London W11

J Pallu & Lake Furnishings Ltd
18 Newman St
London W1P 4AR

Collier Campbell
Fischbacher
(manufacturers)
40-44 Clipstone St
London W1

Collier Campbell fabric also available from decorative fabric wholesalers and retailers throughout the UK

Osborne & Little
304 Kings Road
London SW3 5UH

Marvic Textiles
12-14 Mortimer St
London W1N 7RD

Arthur Sanderson & Sons
Sanderson House
Berners St
London W1P 3AD

Warner & Sons Ltd
Waverley House
7-11 Noel St
London W1V 4AL

Designer's Guild
271 & 277 Kings Road
London SW3 5EN

Charles Hammond
165 Sloane Street
London SW1

Habitat Designs Ltd
196 Tottenham Court Road
London W1

Laura Ashley
183 Sloane Street
London SW1
Branches also throughout the U.K.

Mary Fox Linton
249 Fulham Road
London SW3 6HY

John Lewis Partnership
Oxford St
London W1

Tissunique
10 Princes St
Hanover Sq
London W1

Liberty
Regent St
London W1R 6AH

Colefax & Fowler Designs Ltd
39 Brook St
London W1Y 1AU

Toulemonde Bochart
Divertimenti
139/141 Fulham Road
London SW3

Tamesa Fabrics
343 Kings Road
London SW3

McCulloch & Wallis
25-26 Dering St
London W1R 0BH

Sekers Fabrics Ltd
15-19 Cavendish Place
London W1

Nice Irma's Ltd
46 Goodge St
London W1P 1FJ

Margo International
11 Masons Arms Mews
Maddox St
London W1

Zandra Rhodes

26 Avon Trading Estate
Avonmore Road
London W14

BATHROOMS

Max Pike's Bathroom Shop
4 Eccleston St
London SW1

Czech & Speake Ltd
(reproduction brass taps)
39c Jermyn St
London SW1

Zehnder Radiators
Haenni Ltd
Invincible Rd
Farnborough
Hampshire GU14 7QU

Bonsack Baths
14 Mount St
London W1

West One Bathrooms Ltd
18 North Audley St
London W1

David Hicks Ltd
(Interior Designers)
South Bank Business Centre
Units 8 & 9
1 Ponton Rd
London SW8 5BL

Galleria Montecarlo
66/67 South Audley St
London W1Y 5FE

Sitting Pretty
131 Dawes Rd
London SW6

Architectural Heritage
Boddington Manor
Boddington
Nr Cheltenham
Glos

Armitage Shanks Sales Ltd
Armitage
Rugeley

Staffs WS15 4BT

Bathroom & Shower Centre
204 Great Portland St
London W1N 6AT

Renubath Services
108 Fulham Palace Rd
London W6

Jacuzzi Whirlpool Bath Centre
157 Sloane St
London SW1X 9BT

Mooney Plastics
Unit D
Braintree Trading Estate
Braintree Road
South Ruislip
Middlesex

PAINTS/PAINTING MATERIALS

Wickes DIY Superstores
53 Plough Lane
London SW17
(and other branches)

Sainsbury's Homebase and House & Garden Centre (DIY)
66 Purley Way
Croydon
Surrey
(and other branches)

ICI Paints Division
Wexham Road
Slough
Berkshire SL2 5DS

F A Heffer & Co Ltd
24 The Pavement
London SW4 0JA

John T Keep & Sons Ltd
15 Theobald's Rd
London WC1

Green & Stone
259 Kings Road
London SW3

Simpson's Paints Ltd
354 Edgware Rd
London W2

L. Cornelissen & Sons
Art Colourmen
22 Great Queen St
London WC2

SPECIALIST PAINTERS

Guy Bedford (painted furniture)
Crit Hall
Benedon
Cranbrook
Kent

John Brinklow
4 Flanders Mansions
Flanders Road
London W4 1NE

Lyn le Grice
Catalogue of designs available from:
Alsia Mill
St Buryan
Penzance
Cornwall

Louise Loving (fabric painter)
Studio 2, Unit 4
Charterhouse Works
Eltringham St
London SW18

Fiona Skrine
14 Wilkes Road
London E1

WOOD

W H Newson
481/491 Battersea Park Road
London SW11

Sandell Perkins Plc
57 South Lambeth Road
London SW8 1RJ

BEDS/BEDDING

Futon Company
10-12 Rivington St
London EC2

Sofa Bed Centre
185 Tottenham Court Road
London W1

Sleepeezee Ltd
Morden Road
Merton
London SW19 3XP

Relyon Ltd
Wellington
Somerset TA21 8NN

And So To Bed
638-640 Kings Road
London SW6 2DU

House of Foam
64 Hoe Street
London E17
(foam for making spare beds)

FURNITURE

One Off
56 Neal Street
London WC2

Lancelot Furniture Ltd
Grenville Place
Hale Lane
Mill Hill
London NW7 3SA

Co-existence
17 Canonbury Lane
London N1

Adeptus
110 Tottenham Court Road
London W1

Artemide
(furniture makers)
17-19 Neal St

London WC2

Shaker furniture on display at:
American Museum
Claverton Manor
Bath BA2 7BD

GENERAL STORES

Habitat Design Ltd
196 Tottenham Court Rd
London W1P 9LA

Mothercare
461 Oxford Street
London W1
(branches throughout the UK)

John Lewis Partnership
Oxford Street
London W1
(branches throughout the UK)

Practical Styling
16-18 St Giles High St
London WC2

Astrohome
47-49 Neal St
London WC2

Homeworks
107A Pimlico Road
London SW1

FIREPLACES

Acquisitions
269 Camden High St
London NW1 7BX

The Cast Iron Fireplace Company
103 East Hill
London SW18

Mr Wandle's Workshop
200-202 Garrett Lane

London SW18

Dixons
88 Oxford Street
London W1
(branches throughout the UK)

Acorn Computer Shop
10 Henrietta St
London WC2

FLOORING

Elon Tiles UK Ltd
8 Clarendon Cross
London W11

Amtico
Celanese House
17 St.George's Street
London W1

Shepherd Day Design Association (tiles)
Unit 12
Nimrod Way
Elgar Road
Reading
Berks
(mail order service)

Tiles, Tiles, Tiles
168 Old Brompton Road
London SW5

Tile Mart
151 Great Portland Street
London W1

Nairn Flooring Ltd (vinyl and linoleum)
PO Box 1
Kirkcaldy
Fife
Scotland

BLINDS

Blind Alley Ltd
27 Chalk Farm Road

London NW1

Tidmarsh & Sons
1 Laycock St
London N1 1FW

CURTAINS

Harrison Drapes
PO Box 233
Bradford St
Birmingham

RUGS

The Rug Shop
1 Elystan Street
London SW3 39T

STORAGE

Interlübke
239 Greenwich High Rd
London SE10

ELECTRONICS: COMPUTERS, VIDEOS, TELEVISIONS

Akai (UK) Ltd
12 Silver Jubilee Way
Haslemere
Heathrow Estate
Hounslow

Philips Electronics
Arundel Great Court
8 Arundel St
London WC2R 3DT

Sony UK Ltd
Sony House
South Street
Staines
Middlesex

Tandy Computers

10 Thame Way Tower
Bridge Street
Walsall
West Midlands WS1 1LA

Currys Ltd (head office)
46 Uxbridge Road
London W5
(branches throughout the UK)

UNITED STATES

BEDDING

Simmons International Ltd
6 Executive Park Drive NE
Box 105032
Atlanta
Georgia 30348

John M. McMahon
105 East 16th Street
New York
NY 10003

Windbreaker Trade Link Inc (Zandra Rhodes)
36 West 56th Street
Suite 2C
New York
NY 10019

STORAGE

ICS Inc
305 East 63rd Street
New York 10021

HOUSE BUILDERS

Barratt American Inc
20 Executive Park
Suite 280
PO Box 19646
Irvine

California 92714

FURNITURE MAKERS

Artemide Inc
150 East 58th Street
New York
NY 10155

FURNISHINGS

Ichiro Ohta (oriental)
Tansuya
Ohta Studio Corporation
159 Mercer Street
New York
NY 10012

William Meyer & Associates
(Bauhaus style)
353 East 72nd Street
New York
NY 10021

Yvette Gervey Interiors Inc
(Art Deco)
14 West 75th Street
New York
NY 10023

Furniture on display at:

Shaker Community Inc
PO Box 898
Pittsfield
MA 01201

JACUZZIS, HOT TUBS

California Hot Tubs
60 Third Avenue
New York
NY 10003

AGAS

Russell C Tarr
14 Hatherway Avenue

Beverly
MA 01915

KITCHEN FITTINGS

Bill Norton
Colonel Stephen Ford House
Durham
Connecticut CT 16422

FLOOR TILES

The Tile Shop
1005 Harrison Street
Berkeley
California
CA 94710

BATHS

Baths International
89 Fifth Avenue
New York
NY 10003

Sherle Wagner
60 West 57th Street
New York
NY 10022

FABRICS

Cole & Son
Clarence House
Room 801
111 Eighth Avenue
New York
NY 10011

Martex Textiles
Westpoint Pepperell
1221 Avenue of the Americas
New York
NY 10010

Osborne & Little fabrics
available at:
Brunschwij & Fils Inc
410 East 62nd Street
New York
NY 10573

Collier Campbell fabrics
available from
decorative fabric
wholesalers and retailers
through the U.S.A.

Liberty of London Inc
108 West 39th St
New York
NY 10018

**Colefax & Fowler Designs
Ltd**
Clarence House
Room 801
111 8th Avenue
New York
NY 10011

LIGHTING

Dramatic Lighting Effects
346 West 44th St
New York
NY 10036

Elegant Lighting
1550 Westwood Boulevard
Los Angeles
CA 90024

PAINTS

ICI Americas Inc
Wilmington
Delaware
DE 19897

SPECIALIST PAINTERS

John Canning
132 Meeker road
Southington
CT 06489

GLOSSARY AND BIBLIOGRAPHY

* Words in italic refer to other entries in the glossary.

A

Accent colors Contrast colors, used to enliven a decorative scheme.

Acoustic tiles Tiles made of either a porous mineral fiber or perforated metal trays with glass backing. These tiles absorb sound.

Aga Oven/stove which can provide hot water as well as cook and keep food warm.

Architrave A decorative band that runs around a door, window or panel.

Art Deco New art form, influenced by the 'Arts and Crafts' movement, which spread across Europe in the 1890s. Designers used new materials such as chrome, and the hallmark of their work was elegance and decorative innovation.

B

Baroque Florid extravagant style of art and furnishing in the last half of the seventeenth century.

Batterie de cuisine All the kitchen equipment needed by a cook, from a wooden spoon to a food processor.

Bauhaus German institution for training architects and artists. The Bauhaus doctrine held that there should be no separation between architecture, fine art and applied art.

Broderie anglaise Delicate open embroidery on white linen or cambric.

Builder's store Large store supplying material such as wood and paint to the building trade, and to the public.

Burnt Sienna The pigment in its natural state is brownish yellow, but when 'burnt' takes on an orange glow.

C

Café curtains Two pairs of curtains, one pair on top of another, the lower pair hanging from a pole across the middle of the window.

Carousel shelving Shelving which fits neatly into a cupboard and can be swivelled round for easy access.

Carpet pile The wool or synthetic material which stands up from the base of the carpet.

Chinoiserie Furniture or fabric inspired by Chinese design.

Circotherm Unique to Neff appliances, this is the method by which hot air is circulated inside the oven so that food is cooked evenly. Other kitchen appliance manufacturers have adopted a similar method, called 'convection cooking'.

Combing A wet layer of paint is drawn through evenly with the rigid teeth of a comb to produce vertical stripes.

Console table Small rectangular table which usually stands against a wall.

Corian Simulated white marble.

Cornice Decorative band of molding that runs round the wall of a room, just below the ceiling.

Cubism Revolutionary art movement created between the years 1907-1909 by Picasso and Braque, and heavily influenced by Cézanne. Painting was reduced to mathematical orderliness, and natural forms were geometric shapes.

D

Dado rail A rail fixed to the lower half of the wall some way above the baseboard.

Dhurrie (also dhurry; durry) Indian woven cotton carpet.

Dimmer switch Knob attached to light socket which adjusts the intensity of light in a room.

Distemper Method of painting on plaster or chalk, using colors mixed with egg yolk or size.

Dormer windows Vertical windows which protrude from a sloping roof.

Dowel Metal or wooden pins used to secure and strengthen a joint.

Downlights Recessed spotlights in the ceiling that cast light downward.

Dragging The effect made by dragging a dry brush over wet paint.

E

Eclectic A mixture of different styles and sources of inspiration.

Ergonomics The study of

economical movement. Used in kitchen and bathroom planning to ensure that appliances are within easy reach.

Extractor fan Fan which extracts stale air from a room.

F

Festoon blind A blind which falls into rows of pleats. These look best half way down a window, and they can be coordinated with curtains. Also known as 'ruched' blinds.

Filament lighting Light that is produced by the heating of a small filament within the bulb.

Flocked wallpaper Wallpaper which has a raised patterned surface.

Fluorescent Type of light produced by the fluorescence of gas.

Foam backed A foam backing attached to the floor covering which rules out the necessity of having a separate underlay.

Futon Japanese-style mattress made up of cotton wadding and placed directly onto the floor or onto a mat.

G

Gilding The art of applying gold paint or gold leaf to a piece of furniture or a picture frame.

Gloss Shiny surface produced by oil-based paint.

Gothic Northern European architectural style popular from the twelfth century. Features of the Gothic style include lofty spires, flying buttresses, high and pointed arches and traceried windows. **Graining** Imitation of the natural grains and knots in wood produced by dragging or *ragging* color over the glazed surface of a piece of furniture or wood panneling.

Grouting Filling in cracks, between tiles for example, with a thin mortar.

Gutted An interior which has had everything removed from it, for example the interior walls.

H

Haircord carpet Rough yet durable carpet made from animal hair. It is usually brown in color.

High Tech Decorating style which uses materials and

articles, such as rubber flooring and metal grid shelving, usually found in an industrial setting.

I

Indian jute Fiber used for sacking and mats. It is made from certain plants, chiefly from Bengal.

Industrial shelving system Metal grid shelving usually found in a factory but ideal for storing items in the kitchen.

J

Jacuzzi Bath tub in which jets of aerated water massage the body.

K

Kelim (also kilim) A woven carpet or rug without pile. It is usually reversible.

Kitsch Something which is extremely pretentious, over-elaborate and in questionable taste. It is often used to make a witty 'comment' in a room.

L

Lacquer A hard varnish which is applied in many layers, then polished so that it shines.

Laminate Layers of different substances pressed together and strengthened to make a tough surface material.

Le Corbusier Swiss architect, contributor to the development of the 'International Style' of architecture in the twenties and thirties.

M

Marbling A decorating effect created with a brush or crushed newspaper on wet paint. It imitates the veined and streaked look of real marble.

Matt Flat paint finish with no shine or luster.

Melamine Sprayed-on plastic coating, commonly applied to chipboard to provide a low cost material excellent for shelving.

Microcomputer Desk top computer.

Minimalism Simple, clutter-free style of interior design. No extraneous 'objets d'art'.

Mirror tiles Tiles made from mirror glass or acrylic which can be positioned like ordinary wall tiles.

Miter Neat join of wood or material at 90 degree angle.

Mixer taps Single tap with hot and cold controls.

Modernism The style which makes good use of modern technology and scientifically developed materials.

Modular furniture systems Furniture which can be adjusted and built onto, for example, a bed or storage design.

Moldings The decorative plaster work on cornices or interior arches.

N

Neo Palladian Revival of neoclassical style of sixteenth century Italian architecture.

Night storage heaters Electric heaters which store low cost electricity during the night, then radiate the heat during the day.

O

Open tread stairs Stairs which have no back.

Oven hood A hood over the top of an oven which incorporates an *extractor fan*. Cooking smells are thus removed before they can permeate the room.

P

Pegboard Hardboard perforated with holes. It can be used for giving better acoustics or simply for hanging things from.

Pergola A walkway covered with plants trained over trellis work.

Pillar taps Separate taps raised high above the sink level.

Plastic wood Plastic used to repair wood, which when dry looks like wood.

Plumb line String for testing the perpendicularity of a line.

Polyurethane Plastic resin made to strengthen, for example, varnishes.

Post Modernism A style which like *Minimalism* avoids clutter and fitted furniture, yet attempts to achieve its own iconography with singular design 'statements'.

Pump booster A device to increase the power of the water flowing out of a shower; especially useful at the top of a house where water pressure may be low.

PVC (Polyvinylchloride) A kind of flexible plastic commonly used for clothing or simulated fabric.

Q

Quarry tiles Made from very hard clay, rich in silica and alumina. They are usually square or rectangular.

R

Ragging The three-dimensional effect produced by passing a crumpled rag over wet paint.

Rag rug A rug woven with strips of material to produce a multi-colored effect.

Raw umber A natural pigment, like ocher, but more yellow in color.

Retro A style which harks back to the past, whether it is the eighteenth century or the 1920s.

Ring The top of an oven or stove on which the gas burners or electric hot plates are positioned. The ring can be detached from the oven and built into a work surface.

S

Sanding Smoothing with a rough sandpaper.

Scumbling A variant on *stippling*: an opaque coat is stippled over a bright and shiny base color with a dry brush. This technique is best used on furniture.

Seal A preparation used on a surface to protect it from water penetration, wear and tear.

Shakers Eighteenth century Quaker community who fled religious persecution in England, and set up self-sufficient communities in North America. The furniture that they made has become renowned for its simplicity and purity of line.

Software The programs run on computers (which are termed the 'hardware').

Spattering Spraying paints in different colors onto wet paint to create a multi-colored leopard-skin look.

Spirit level Glass tube partly filled with spirit to test whether a surface is horizontal; if it is, the bubble in the spirit will be in the middle.

Splashplate The tiled back to a sink or vanity unit that prevents water from penetrating the wall.

Sponging Applying layer after layer of paint with a sponge, usually combining opaque and translucent colors.

Stenciling The art of tracing patterns through the holes in a block of wood, card or metal.

Stippling A grainy texture applied upon wet paint by dry brushes or a dry roller.

Stove black Special paint for stoves and cast-iron fire surrounds.

Surrealist A style arising from the Surrealist movement in modern art. Surrealism seeks to shock the beholder by juxtaposing reality with unreality, as seen in the weird paintings of Salvador Dali.

Swag Elaborate treatment for hanging curtains so that the material falls in a series of graceful curves.

T

Task lighting Lighting for a particular purpose: for example, a strip of fluorescent light under a cupboard in a kitchen can illuminate the main work surface area.

Tongue and groove Boarding which neatly fits together, 'tail' to 'head'.

Track lighting Lights attached to a metal track so that they can be moved about.

Tumble dryer, condenser The dryer contains a medium which condenses the water vapor inside the machine and expels the water into a pipe.

Tumble dryer, direct vent A dryer directly vented to the outside so that water vapor is instantly expelled from the room.

Tungsten light Lighting in which a filament inside the light bulb heats up to create light.

V

Valance The frill around the base of a bed to hide the divan, or a short drapery to conceal the top of curtains and fixtures.

VDU Visual Display Unit — the TV screen on a computer.

Venetian blinds Blinds made up of slats of wood or plastic that can be turned to exclude or admit more light.

Vinyl Tough, yet malleable plastic used for easy-to-clean floor coverings.

W

Wash color Pigment mixed with water applied over an emulsion base paint.

Whirlpool jet tub Another name for a *jacuzzi*.

Wood-burning stove These are becoming popular again, and are available as antique or reproduction furniture.

BIBLIOGRAPHY

Books
Affordable Splendour Diana Phipps, Weidenfeld and Nicolson
Living in Style Jocasta Innes, Ebury Press
The Complete Home Book Pamela Ferguson, Quarto, New York
Encyclopaedia of Decorative Arts 1890-1940 Phaidon Press
The Decorating Book Mary Gilliatt, Michael Joseph

Periodicals
Kitchen Guide, House and Garden, UK
Bathroom Guide, House and Garden, UK
La Maison de Marie Claire, France
Avenue, Holland
The Sunday Times Colour supplement June 3rd, 1984: Georgina Howell writing about style
Options, UK
The World of Interiors, UK

INDEX

Page numbers in *italic* refer to captions and illustrations.

221

ACKNOWLEDGEMENTS

Interviews with decorators, designers and architects are the cornerstone of this book, so my list of acknowledgements begins with a thank-you to Judy Brittain, editor of the 'Living' pages in British 'Vogue' who commissioned me in the first place to collect information from many sources for her pages. Among the many designers who contributed their working plans and ideas to this book, I would like to thank in particular Susan Collier and Sarah Campbell – their great sense of style can be seen in their textile designs on the front cover, and throughout the book; Tricia Guild of Designer's Guild for her inspiration on colour; David Hersey, the theatrical lighting expert for Broadway and West End musicals, whose patient explanations of the principles and practicalities of lighting in the home clarified a complex subject. My special thanks to the art editor at Quarto, Nick Clark, for making the book beautiful as well as practical; to editors Emma Johnson and Lucinda Montefiore for shaping the book into its present readable form; to Catherine Carpenter for editing the American edition; to Keith Bernstein for picture research; and to team-mates from the 'Brides and Setting Up Home' magazine days; Christine Knox who collected the fabric swatches from many sources, and Anne Holker who helped to compile captions and the directory of suppliers, working at speed with good humour and professionalism. Pictures from many sources are credited elsewhere but I would like to single out for my thanks those publicity officers and public relations officers who helped to produce working drawings and photographs for this book: Sheila Fitzjohns, Juliette Hellman and David· Farquhar, Fiona Wiley of Tina Caprez Associates, and Barbara Lovett of Paul Winner Marketing Communications. I would also like to thank the following photographers who were particularly helpful: Christine Hanscomb, Karen Bussolini, John Vaughan, Michael Dunne, John Wyand, Michael Boys and Ken Kirkwood.